FIGHTING THE INVISIBLE ENEMY

Know the Weapons
of Your Spiritual Warfare

DAVID D. WEL

A Note from the Publisher

The publisher wishes to acknowledge and thank Dr Douglas H. Johnson for his invaluable help and support for Africa World Books and its mission of preserving and promoting African cultural and literary traditions and history. Dr Johnson and fellow historians have been instrumental in ensuring that African people remain connected to their past and their identity. Africa World Books is proud to carry on this mission.

© D. Wel, 2021

ISBN: 978-0-6451109-2-0

All rights reserved.

No part of this publication may be reproduced, stored in a retrieval system, or transmitted, in any form, or by any means, electronic, mechanical, photocopying, recording or otherwise, without the prior permission of the publishers.

This book is sold subject to the conditions that it shall not, by way of trade or otherwise, be lent, re-sold, hired out or otherwise circulated without the publisher's prior consent in any form of binding or cover other than in which it is published and without a similar condition including the condition being imposed on the subsequent purchaser.

Cover design, typesetting and layout : Africa World Books

DEDICATION

This book is dedicated to; those believers who have been victims of the spiritual warfare, and those who are now undergoing spiritual warfare, and those who will go under the spiritual warfare in future and who will be helped by this book to turn their lives around for the better. I wrote this book with full confidence that the ideas in it have helped us as the family and there is no reason whatsoever, that these ideas cannot help you in your struggles, in life now and in the future.

CONTENTS

Acknowledgements	7
Foreword	9
Prologue	13
Introduction	17
Chapter 1: The Nature of The Battle and The Battlefield	23
Chapter 2: Confession, Repentance and Baptism of The Holy Spirit	45
Chapter 3: Name and Blood of our Lord Jesus Christ	55
Chapter 4: Prayer	65
Chapter 5: Fasting	86
Chapter 6: The Shield of Faith	94
Chapter 7: The Belt of Truth	102
Chapter 8: The Breastplate of Righteousness	109
Chapter 9: The Shoes of Peace	114
Chapter 10: The Helmet of Salvation	120
Chapter 11: The Sword of Spirit	130
Chapter 12: Breaking the Demonic Strongholds in Your Life and Your Family	137
Bibliography	150

ACKNOWLEDGEMENTS

"The God of heaven, nothing I am prouder than the God I worship and serve." To apply the knowledge, abilities, and skills, in writing this book I had to seek God for his wisdom and understanding." Yes indeed, many people in the world today think that they can still be great without him, but that is to the world standards. But if you want to be very great, then you must seek God's standards, including his salvation which is priceless.

To My dear wife Rachel Awuok Ayuel, you have been the great force behind everything I do including writing this book. Although we continue to face challenges on the most important aspects of our lives, that makes a complete family, you continue to defy all odds to stick by me. Even today when the forces of darkness are trying to break us apart, I am sure we will overcome them. Because nothing breaks the zeal of people who have a united vision and mission in life. You promised me a little under ten (10) years ago, when you gave your hand in marriage to me, to stick by me whether in good or bad times. The case which I was not sure by then that we will fall into a big one, which continues to foreshadow and threatens our togetherness today. You have done more for me than a husband should have asked and expect from a wife. Thank you so much for that.

I am also grateful to St Paul Church; staff and particularly pastor Timon Yanga, for having allowed me to serve God in the senior capacity of the church as a preacher and as well as a Warden. Your support has without a doubt strengthened my Christian calling and my duty to worship and serve the living God. I acknowledged your desire to train future leaders of the church including myself. But not only that but also the previous training you made available to other preachers of the word of God and me, which has allowed me to launch deep into the word of God and to study even more for my sermons. Your help has given me a complete understanding and clear picture of Christ call in my life.

FOREWORD

This Book Serves as My Personal Testimony of Spiritual Warfare

I wrote this book as a victim of spiritual warfare. I have gone through many catastrophes in my life starting at a young age, with little knowledge or no knowledge of whether I was under spiritual attack. I was a battleground between the forces of light (God) versus the forces of darkness (Satan). The demonic forces attempted on many occasions to eliminate me from the face of the earth through; thunderstorm (1986), scorpion bites (1988), near-missed capture by rebels (1991), near-missed shot at by gunman (2002), and near-missed plane crash (2011). Through all these, Satan was actively trying to blot my name off this earth. Furthermore, in 2011, I got married to my wife Rachel, and we ran into difficulty in which we are not able to conceive a child without apparent natural or medical reasons. This was the final attempt by the devil on my life. Given the expectations in any marriage, it is too difficult to sustain a marriage without children, which is also a recipe for disaster for many couples, but by God mercy, we are fighting on. Shockingly as it may be to us to be without children, it has become a turning point for us to seek God and his intervention. Now that we have found God, I know with absolute certainty that one day we will have children of our own by God's grace.

Despite all these attempts by the devil on my life, I am protected by the alternative force I did not know at that time but now know as the Holy Spirit of God. At a very young age I had struggled with inward self-generating questions such as these; What will your life be after this life? How do you live a life of which you do not know the ending when you die? "These questions at such a young age caused me to think that life is meaningless, worthless and without hope. "Little did I know that it was the spirit of God preparing me for a future role in spreading the gospel of the Lord Jesus Christ.

Surprisingly, in August 2017, we collectively heard a voice while in deep sleep at our home, telling us the opposite of what we were told by the medical institutions, that we will have children. It was a nice calm and gentle voice of love from the father of creation (God). This voice without a doubt had injected back into our lives a hope of the future in a hopeless and senseless situation of despair. As we were in a deep sleep that night, we could not speak to each other, but when we woke up in the morning, we excitedly rushed to tell each other the version of the good news in a voice we had received that night. Without a doubt, as we know it was the voice of the Holy Spirit. This voice of the Holy Spirit has brought confidence and assurance that the solution to our problem is in the hands of God almighty, and at any time from now we will celebrate the victory of God over Satan in our lives. While we are waiting for that victory we are encouraging and comforting ourselves by listening to many great men of God teachings, reading Christian books, reading the bible, praying, and fasting, to enrich ourselves with the knowledge, wisdom and understanding of God and his ways. Contrastingly, this became our departure from the natural world (physical world) into the spiritual world (unseen world); the spirit of God (Holy Spirit) became actively engaged with us through the deep revelations of the verses of the bible, word of knowledge, voice, dreams, and visions of the night.

Just as this book is a wakeup called in our lives about spiritual warfare, it will act also as a wakeup call for those who are already going through difficult moments of their lives and those who will go through difficult moments in their lives in the future.

I joined this war against Satan not to be complacent. I joined to make a difference in the lives of those who are oppressed by him. So, my job now is to expose the devil as much as possible. Nothing more or less than this. Satan is real just as you are real but in another realm. The difference is that you cannot see him, but he is seeing you because he is a spirit without a body.

I am now a passionate preacher and teacher of the word of God, to bring hope to hopeless people through it. It is very difficult, if not impossible to have hope after one has gone either through drug addiction, life-threatening disease, childlessness, divorce, financial breakdown, a business collapse, deceit, starvation, war, corruption, hate, poverty, abuse, imprisonment, loss of an important family member, depression, anxiety, devastating natural disasters and all other forms of injustice and the inequality in the today society. It is my sincere belief that all these things do not just happen to us. There is a real enemy: the devil and his demons who are against our God-given future. The bible makes this clear that we are in a battle not against our fellow human beings but against principalities, against powers, against the rulers of the darkness of this age, against spiritual hosts of wickedness in the heavenly places *(Ephesians 6:12)*.

When we were created by God, we were meant to be safeguarded and protected by him, but we chose to go it alone without him. In today's world we look for joy, love, peace and happiness in our jobs, possessions, and relationships which we pursue with vigour but to little avail. It is only through seeking God and his protection that we can have a meaningful life of love, peace, and joy in this dangerous world. In a nutshell, we were made to know and to walk with God in our life journey on earth, but we rejected him. Do not be deceived, King Solomon had it all, but he never had happiness, and neither will you without God. Turn to God and live a happy life. Put Jesus Christ first in your life and watch how he will turn it around for good. It is only by doing that you will discover that him alone, can give you the love, peace, joy, and happiness that you want in abundance in this life now on earth.

There is even more to this as I just lately discovered that God as our creator has a plan for us. We were created by God with great potential within us and it is my determination to help you discover your God-given gift within you. For you to increase your productivity, I will help you unlock your potential by bringing resources, information, knowledge, wisdom and understanding to you for you to live and enjoy the life you were born to live.

Power of the information: the information you lack or the information you have, and you do not apply in your life, is what will destroy you.

***DAVID WEL** holds a master's degree of International Business and a Master's Degree of National Security and International Relations from Edith Cowan and Curtin Universities in Perth, Australia.*

PROLOGUE

Once you become a born-again Christian there is a battle over your soul by the enemy of your soul called Satan. This battle is called spiritual warfare, fought with spiritual weapons in the spiritual realm. The reason why it is called spiritual warfare is that it is fought in the spirit, the unseen spiritual world.

With this in mind, it is important to bring to your attention the location of the battle, which I referred to above as the spiritual realm. And before that, if I may ask you for the sake of testing your knowledge, where is the spiritual realm? Some people may have a clear picture of the location some people may not. Well, St. Paul gives us the answer in the book of; ***Ephesians 6:10-12- "Finally, my brethren, be strong in the Lord and in the power of His might. Put on the whole armour of God, that you may be able to stand against the wiles of the devil. For we do not wrestle against flesh and blood, but against principalities, against powers, against the rulers of the darkness of this age, against spiritual hosts of wickedness in the heavenly places."***

The phrase here, "we don't wrestle against flesh and blood" tells us that our war is not with our fellow human beings. The battle is not against our spouse, co-workers, children, friends, and neighbours but against Satanic angels based in the heavenly places (also called second heaven). People are conduits used by demons directed by superior angels based in the second heaven to secure their domination of earth to the disadvantage of humankind. Satan and his demons cannot execute their agenda on earth unless they have found a human body to use to steal, kill and destroy our fellow human beings. That is why you and I are the target of the devil to use against our fellow human beings. It is important to know that Satan is trying to fight off God's influence over human beings in order for him to control the whole earth without God. But not only that, he wants to take away our God-given blessings over our lives. If you do not realise that Satan exists-then he has already controlled, you and your blessings. But he has no reason to do that because he did not create you -you are God's. When God created you and placed you on the earth, he created you with your blessings intact within you which the devil is trying to take away from you. Perhaps this book is giving you an opportunity for your eyes to be opened and rise to the challenge of fighting for your freedom with your God-given weapons.

I can tell you without reservation that there is spiritual warfare against Christians which can only be fought and won with spiritual weapons, not physical weapons. Unless you know your spiritual weapons, you cannot win this spiritual warfare. All the wars we fight today in the natural world in all forms are directed and decided against us in the spiritual world. "Whether it is, for example, any sickness, or natural disasters, human hatreds, or wars and conflicts, they are first decided and directed to us from the invisible world to the visible world." So, what we see happening in the physical world, has first been set in motion against us in the supernatural world. As a matter of fact, things are not accidents-they just do not happen to us from anywhere. Unless you have dealt with the roots of all your problems in the invisible world, you cannot win the war in the visible world of the problems you are going through. The bible tells us that the wars we go through today in the world started in heaven between God and his angels against Lucifer (Satan) and his angels. Lucifer (Satan) and his angels lost the war in heaven and were cast to the earth. This must be a big bombshell to many people who are not aware that Satan is with us here on earth. Although he operates from second heaven, he has his representatives here on earth called demons, who can possess human bodies including your body if you are not a born-again Christian. Hence, there is a battle of ownership of your body by these demons to carry out their boss (Satan's) agenda on earth.

There are many dangerous positions Christians take about the existence of Satan which includes denial of his existence or the underestimation of the danger he poses to them. The former makes them vulnerable to the devil's attacks and the latter lets him destroy their vision and mission. There are limited choices in this if there are any for Christians not to believe that there is a war being directed against them. Duly pose and ponder on these;

- If there is no war then Jesus Christ would not have been crucified on the cross,
- If there is no war St. Paul could not have referred to Christians, as soldiers,
- If there is no war St. Paul would not have talked about the weapons of our spiritual warfare as Christians,
- If there is no war, then Cain would not have killed his own brother Abel,
- If there is no war, then St. Peter would not have cut off high Priest's servant's ear,
- If there is no war then we would not go through life-threatening illnesses, bitter family divorce, financial difficulty, hatred, jealousy, starvation, natural disasters, wars and so many more troubles in our world today.

The battle over our bodies, souls, and spirits by these spiritual forces can be summed up as follows: God is not willing that anyone should perish, whereas Satan is not willing that anyone should be saved. To me, this looks like a war over our souls and spirits between the two kingdoms. This conflict is played out practically in a person's life, during temptation. Let me start with this statement-It is one thing to declare yourself a winner of war before you go to war, but it is another to declare yourself a winner of war after you have been to war. This is so true with many Christians today, who claim that the devil is powerless against them when they have not actually faced demonic attacks. The main reasons among others, why we come under God trials and Satanic temptations sometimes may be; firstly, the fact that we are sitting on God's assignment, which we are not aware of. It is important to note that God test to build while Satan tempt to destroy. Here God, allow trials our ways, to test our faith, in order to see whether we are up to the task and to also act as a wakeup call to be aware of his intention to reveal himself to us. Secondly, Satan tempts us because we may have been dedicated to him in the past and he tempts what he owns. Thirdly, it may be that we have been sinning continuously without repentance, of which we fall into Satan temptations. This is a very dangerous one, if you do not repent and turn to God, Satan will destroy you (kill you).

The shocking reality to many Christians today, if truth be told, is that many of them do not know how to fight spiritual warfare even if they believe there is a spiritual war. This book will open your eyes and connect you to the supernatural world like never before and it will also change your thinking about the physical wars we fought today in the world. You will know the tricks, tactics, and ways in which these wars are engineered and directed against you from the spiritual world. All these wars come from the same location (supernatural world), whether they are directed against individuals, communities, societies, or nations. Unless you pay close attention to the supernatural world you will never win a war in the natural world. Unless you have dealt with the root causes of everything you are facing in the supernatural world, you will only be dealing with the symptoms in the natural world. For example, you cannot claim to have destroyed the tree unless you have dealt with its roots. Doctors cannot treat the disease unless they have found the cause. That is also the same way you must approach the problem you are going through. Everything has a cause and effect.

It is only in the Bible that you can understand the root causes of all diseases, family divorce, family childlessness, financial crisis, drunkenness, starvation, natural disasters, wars, hatred, jealousy, lying, cheating, and so much more. The world has no answers and explanations to all of these and particularly their root causes. What people do is react to them by attempting to address the symptoms, but not the root causes. In the same context, you cannot win a war against yourself, family, community, society, and nations until you have dealt with roots in the supernatural. To this effect, the only way you know there is spiritual war decided and directed against you somewhere is when for a few minutes you are a happy person and in the next few minutes, you are a sorrowful person. This is an indication that you have no control over your life and what happens to you. This is exactly why we cannot explain the mysteries of the world we live in as human beings. The only way we can understand and explain them is through the word of God-the Bible. The Bible is not a history book as many Christians turn to believe but a life of Christians-as it tells all that there is in this world.

INTRODUCTION

As every year comes and passes by, arm yourself with the mindset that, we as Christians are in a war with Satan. The world we are born in, live in and die in, is not a safer place as we think. The bible talks about this war in the book of; ***Revelations 12:7-12- "And war broke out in heaven: Michael and his angels fought with the dragon; the dragon and his angels fought, but they did not prevail, nor was a place found for them in heaven any longer. So the great dragon was cast out, that serpent of old, called the Devil and Satan, who deceives the whole world; he was cast to the earth, and his angels were cast out with him. Then I heard a loud voice saying in heaven, "Now salvation, and strength, and the kingdom of our God, and the power of His Christ have come, for the accuser of our brethren, who accused them before our God day and night, has been cast down. "And they overcame him by the blood of the Lamb and by the word of their testimony, and they did not love their lives to the death. "Therefore rejoice, O heavens, and you who dwell in them! Woe to the inhabitants of the earth and the sea! For the devil has come down to you, having great wrath, because he knows that he has a short time."***

When God created human beings, he placed them in a dangerous territory, which is infested by Satan. The war we fight today in the world began in heaven between God and Satan. According to the book of Ezekiel 28, Lucifer (who became Satan) was the most anointed and decorated angel created by God. "You were the anointed cherub who covers; I established you; You were on the holy mountain of

God; You walked back and forth in the midst of fiery stones. You were perfect in your ways from the day you were created, till iniquity was found in you. **(Ezekiel 28:14-15).** He decided to rebel against God in heaven (because he wanted to be like God) and took one-third of the angels of God with him, as he had lost the battle in heaven and was cast to the earth. God as a result had to create human beings in his own image (Adam and Eve) and placed them on earth to take care and control God's creation on earth. This action by God even annoyed Satan the most and he had to response against God. Contrastingly, Satan had to counter that by getting Adam and Eve to rebel against God as well and he took control of God property (the earth).

God provided his redemptive move by kicking Adam and Eve out of the garden of Eden and lest they can eat from the tree of life for them to become permanent rebels against God like Satan. Satan countered the move by getting Cain to kill Abel to cut off God's relationship with humanity through the contamination of humans' genetics of the generations to follow. God responded by getting Adam and Eve to give birth again to a clean seed (Seth). Satan countered the move by getting Nimrod to build the Tower of Babel thinking that he would be higher than God. And the battle had to continue through Abraham, Moses, David, Jesus Christ until today.

But God had to end this battle finally by sending his own son to die on the cross to give final and last victory and freedom to those who would later believe in him. By the crucifixion of Jesus Christ on the cross, Satan thought he had defeated God and his plan of the redemption of humanity. But the God-plan to raise Jesus Christ from death on behalf of humanity, was so that those who will believe in him will have life through him. This was a final move by God to defeat Satan once and for all on behalf of humanity to restore us to himself. As we live today on earth, God's victory on our behalves for our battle has been won and secured for us through Christ's victory on the cross against Satan.

But let make this clear, even as the battle has been won Satan continues to deceive, intimidate, and kill those who reject Jesus Christ and those who are not sure of this victory. Someone may ask Why is this? Well, until judgement day Satan continues to rule the world given to him through Adam and Eve. But this is a limited power allowed by God until Satan is taken out of earth shortly after the return of our Lord Jesus Christ to rule the earth with those who believe in him. So, Satan continues to have considerable power over those who reject the Son of God as a propitiation for their sins. This must be a warning to those who may die without God, that if they die, they will be dead forever, as nothing will take away their sins. The reason God had to raise Jesus Christ from the dead was that he was sinless, and there was nothing against him from Satan to keep him in hell. What about you? What will keep you out of hell if not Jesus Christ, whom God has assigned to us as a means of our salvation?

We are in a fight as long as Satan and demons are still operating here on earth. They are planning to bring destruction against you and your family, no matter what day, month, and year you are in. You must be circumspectly alert. You must fight a good fight of faith if you are to survive here on earth. The reality that there is God and the devil, assures us that there is a battle between the two spirits over the control of humanity. This battle is being fought over you as a person whether you like it or not. Whether you have noticed or not it comes to this choice; Choosing God is choosing life now in these physical bodies, and in the spiritual bodies to come, and choosing the devil is choosing death now in these physical bodies, and in the spiritual bodies to come. We must not seek God when we are about to die. How good is that to God? Think about that!!! We must be active, not reactive Christians. This means that you must not wait to be hit by the devil with disaster to seek God. Despite humanity's advancements in areas of science and technology, Satan continues to beat us back through natural disasters, death, wars, and all forms of human sufferings. God allows you to go through problems so that you can know he exists and to let others know also that he exists through the manifestation of his power over your problems. The reason why God cannot stop the devil attacks over your life is to allow you to experience the badness of the devil so that you can turn to him.

When people rebel against God the alternative is the devil who goes and points them away from their true creator. Science is one of those areas of human society heavily influenced by the devil today that would have us believe that humans originated from apes. It is not only science alone but other sources of information that fail to acknowledge God as the creator of human beings and the universe they live in. This indicates that there is a war over the information you get from every source including the bible. The reason so many people have rejected the bible today is the fact that there are other sources of information available to them that point to other gods, rather than the true God. Therefore, this book is important to you, to read, to digest, and to bring correct thinking in making clear choices for your life in this confusing world. I made a choice to believe the bible because it explains clearly to me the origin of the universe including myself when no other sources convinced me, and it makes sense to me and that is why I believed it. The secondary or the alternative information Adam received from Satan destroyed him. And this was it. Did God say, you will not eat from the tree of knowledge of good and evil? Adam yes. Satan, it is a lie, for if you eat from the tree of knowledge good and evil you will be like God. Adam acted on half-true and half-lie information; because he believes the lie from the devil that he can be like God, and so he believed and took the information as truth. He began to know things he should not have known and began to feel ashamed. Because it was a piece of half- lie information, having eaten from the tree of knowledge of good and evil, he never became like God. Instead, he received a penalty for rebellion against himself and the rest of his offspring's. Humanity was deceived by Satan. This is still true today the secondary information we received from a secondary source (the world) is the one that will destroy us mankind. We have become too clever for God, we think, and have educated ourselves out of God sources of Knowledge such as the bible. This is Perhaps: many people in our world today do not believe there is God, some are not sure, and some worship religion more than God. This is why the current world is destined for destruction.

By contrast, you cannot explain this war until you get to the bottom of it, dealing with the invisible enemy-this is how the whole thing came into play. 'Death came into the world through sin by one man (our great grandfather, Adam)."Committing sin is the perfect opportunity for Satan to get into your affairs with or without your full knowledge and start ripping off your future. This is exactly what happened to Adam and Eve and continues to happen to us today. The Devil tries to get you to commit sins in the following areas-marriage, job, business, finances, power, and leadership in order to get to you. God, when he had created humans, he did not want them to know his bad part including knowing Satan's existence. This brings us to the concept of the tree of knowledge of good and evil. 'This literally means knowing "good" and knowing "bad" at the same time. 'But also, in deeper terms means knowing God and knowing Satan at the same time. No single human being on this planet will not acknowledge that these forces of good and bad plays out practically within themselves. We can choose to do good or bad according to what we choose at that moment in time. We are faced with these choices of good and bad in our daily lives, yet we try to brush them aside as if nothing is happening. For example, every Sunday we are faced with two choices of going to church to worship or not. If we choose to go to church then we have chosen to go to the house of God to worship him and if we choose not to, then we chose to be away from God. It may be as simple as that. 'What you worship as your God, that is what Satan will try to destroy you with. 'What tree of knowledge of good and evil do you worship? What do you believe to be more important to you than God, that has pulled you away from God and outside God? Is it your relationship, job, education, wealth, or power? What is it that has occupied and has taken your time, making you not to have time for God?

In a few words "Fighting The Invisible Enemy" is the title of this book. It can be summed up this way, things such as; drug addiction, diseases, childlessness, divorce, poverty, business failure, deceit, starvation, war, corruption, greed, hate, poverty, abuse, imprisonment, premature loss of loved ones, depression, anxiety, devastating natural disasters and all other forms of the human society injustices and inequality are all works of the invisible enemy (Satan). The fact that we do not control any of these things shows that someone else somewhere is controlling and directing them against us. Is it not time to get up and fight back for your freedom? If you understand this statement, then it will change your thinking forever about this world and your very existence in it. Every source of new information to you including this book will save your life.

Listen to this very carefully, "your adversary," is your hater and accuser. If you are a Christian, then you must know that you have a dangerous spy against you and your way of life. For him to block your blessings or even to kill you for that matter, he must have a strong case against you in the presence of God in heaven. While you are awake or asleep, he is there accusing you before God in heaven. He is so determined to bring you down at all costs to destroy your salvation. To do this he has to file a case against you on a daily basis over whatever you think, speak, and do that is wicked in nature. He lost his place in heaven, and he does not want you to go to heaven. With this in mind, you are either a Christian or not a Christian at all. If you want to be a tough Christian who can win against the devil, then you must always shun sins. There are no double standards in Christian life. If you think that the life of a Christian is a simple life, then think again.

Isn't it a foolishness to wait until you are under attack to believe there is God and Satan?

Chapter 1

The Nature of The Battle and The Battlefield

The Nature of the Battle

We have seen the nature of war as spiritual warfare, but we must also know where it is fought. This is very important for you as a soldier. The nature of this war is spiritual. We know that something spiritual is anything that cannot be seen. The war is fought in another world called the second heaven or the spiritual realm. Second heaven according to the bible is the home of the fallen angels, headed by Satan himself. *(Ephesians 2:2).* These powerful angels who lost the war in the third heaven (home of God), are based in the second heaven and ruled the world by proxy – the demons who possessed our bodies to carry out their senior angels' agenda on earth. These spirits called demons have no ability to fly because they are offspring of Satanic angels who procreated with the sons and daughters of mankind shortly before the destruction of the earth by flood. Hence, they travel and loiter the earth looking for bodies to possess to carry out their Satanic agenda on earth.

This war is planned and directed against human beings from the second heaven (unseen spiritual world) but is waged against us in the physical world (the seen world). Even though the causes of the war are from the unseen realm, its effects are clearly seen and felt here on earth. In a nutshell, almost every problem we face in the natural (physical world), has a root cause in the spiritual (the unseen) world. Let me put it another way. Everything physical has spiritual causes or it is influenced by the spiritual world. For a person to win the war in the physical realm he must fight the war in the spiritual realm. In other words, every person must deal with the roots of every problem he faces in the physical world whatever the size.

It must be made clear that the war we fought in the physical world must not be against flesh and blood but against Satanic spiritual powers in the spiritual realm. To be exact the war we fight almost every day in the physical world against our fathers, mothers, brothers, sisters, co-workers, leaders, and all the people we labelled as our enemies are incited, influenced, and flamed by the demonic forces to achieve their own agenda through us. So, we always fight the war we do not know against our fellow human beings, directed through us by the spiritual powers that are working in us and through us. This must act as a flashlight to you today if you are a quick-tempered person who loves fighting. To be clear your enemy is not your fellow human being but the demonic powers at work in you to aid their agenda without you being aware. In brief, your fight should be directed against these spiritual rulers, and powers of darkness located in the heavenly places. Heavenly places again mean the spiritual realm (the unseen world). In these verses of the bible St. Paul put it very clearly: ***Finally, my brethren, be strong in the Lord and in the power of His might. Put on the whole*** *armour* ***of God, that you may be able to stand against the wiles of the devil. For we do not wrestle against flesh and blood, but against principalities, against powers, against the rulers of the darkness of this age, against spiritual hosts of wickedness in the heavenly places. (Ephesians 6:10-12).***

Behind every physical attack over your body or that of your close relatives, whether it is sickness, wars, natural disasters, poverty, depression, suicide, lust, alcoholism, drug addiction, oppression, divorce, financial breakdown, homosexuality, adultery, molestations, fornication, strangling and all other forms of attack, they are directed against you in the supernatural world. You can now see for yourselves how deadly the spiritual world is against the physical world. One thing you must not let go of while reading this book is that everything you see in the physical is not all that there is – this is very important indeed for your life and the battle over your life by the enemy. Here is a very important point to take home; what has gone on, is going on and will go on in your life in the future is rooted in the spiritual realm. Unless you have dealt with the spiritual realm you will never win this war in the physical realm.

What Satan does not want you to know is the fact that there is another world where the physical world can be impacted from. Satan will be happy if indeed he can keep you in a loop of confusion from this reality. When this happens, he can destroy you as much as he wants but with no or little knowledge of what is happening in your life and how to overcome it. He wants you to operate through your five senses; what you hear, what you see, what you taste, what you touch, and what you smell is all he wants you to know. If he can divert your attention away from the spiritual realm then he is a winner over your life, which is a recipe for him to steal, kill and destroy your life and your properties. Now is the time to wake up to this reality that there is another world which is a deadly world to your own very existence on earth.

The Battlefield is Your Body

Before I go deep into the details about this battlefield, can I ask you this question; who is your enemy? Many people will answer this question differently, but I guess your answer will be along these lines; my enemy is a person who has a plan to do me harm – both physical and spiritual. It can be a person who howls verbal abuse at me or a person who assaults me physically.

But Have You Asked Why He is Doing it to You?

Again, many people will have different answers to this question, but the answers will be along these lines; he is doing it to me because I have wronged him, or he has wronged me. Sometimes when the issue is too remote, many people will say, they do not know why people behave nicely or badly towards them. Whatever the case there are always reasons why people behave differently toward you or others based on their own underlying issue within them. Sometimes people hate you because of the way you think, the way you talk and the way you act. Well, I can tell you now, there is a spiritual force behind the way we respond towards others and others towards us. The bible tells us that what comes out of us is influenced or directed by spiritual forces present inside us against others. On many occasions, our responses towards others or others towards us, whether we like it or not, are influenced or flamed by the spiritual forces within us. Our Lord Jesus Christ put it very well in these verses of the Bible; ***"But those things which proceed out of the mouth come from the heart, and they defile a man. 'For out of the heart proceed evil thoughts, murders, adulteries, fornications, thefts, false witness, blasphemies. These are the things which defile a man, but to eat with unwashed hands does not defile a man." (Matthew 15:18-20).***

Note this, "Out of our hearts proceed evil thoughts." What we think in many cases is influenced by the devil with or without our full knowledge. This puts the battle squarely on you and me.

Why is the Battlefield Over Your Body?

For the spirits to work and operate here on earth they need your body. For them to carry out their agenda on earth they need a human body. That is why immediately before Noah's flood Satanic angels came and procreated with the sons and daughters of mankind to poison the whole generation of mankind to rebel against God. The position of Satan is that he wants to make sure that no single human being on earth calls on the name of God. Satan wants to be worshipped. In fact, the reason he rebelled against God in heaven was over the issue of worship. He wants to be worshipped by human beings on earth. Once he possesses or can influence you through the demons, he wants to make sure that you lose your ability to worship God. The reason among others that he wants to infiltrate and impact the world, or even possible to change it from being God's property to being his own property, is so that he makes sure that he possesses individuals, families, churches, and societies to worship him.

Satan Servants

Have you ever asked yourself why we have today in the world: sorcerers, diviners, magicians, witch doctors, palm readers, fortune tellers and mediums? Have you asked who are they for if Satan is not real? Have you ever investigated what they do? Well, I want you to know today that these people are agents of Satan. They are here on earth to bring destruction to your lives. Without God, nothing could protect you from their practices. They are determined to steal, kill, and destroy your God-given destiny. They do devil bidding over your lives. They want to recruit as many people into their camp as much as possible. They want to influence your life to commit sin in order for God to reject you and to join them in the rebellion against God. They know by doing this God will curse you and to live a cursed life here on earth, when you die you will join them in hell. That is all the business for Satan and his demons on earth. I usually say and we will continue to say again that there are only two kingdoms running the affairs of the earth as namely, God kingdom and the Satanic Kingdom. Whether you know it or not you fall into any of these two kingdoms.

The fact that Satan servants are present in our human societies today tells you that Satan is alive and well. These agents are present in every area of human society such as politics, media, business, cultures, traditions, science, church, education, and the medical institutions. Their job is to divide people against each other so that there is no human progress. It is either you are with them or you will never succeed. They breed among the people of nations and societies violence, hatred, division, tribalism, corruption, greed, slavery, bitterness, idolatry, bondage, anger, and antichrist movements. Furthermore, people have ended up in prisons and in mental health facilities across nations, who should not have been there because of these demons. As I keep saying there are no crazy human beings apart from, the ones who are captives of the devil and his demons.

Let me bring to your attention the following strongholds of the devil and his demonic influence over your lives for you to see whether you are already captives of Satan. The purpose of these categorisations is in order for you to examine yourself critically, and if you are honest you will know that at least there is already an area in your life that is the stronghold of the devil if not many. At least if you are honest, there will be one area in your life that is out of control in the below list. Accepting these facts will not only pose to you the dangers of Satan but also force you to seek Jesus Christ as the solution to your problems. Below is the list of satanic influence over our lives according to the great man of God **John Ramirez**:

- **Witchcraft/occultic practices-** Fortune telling, Spiritual healer, Psychics, Shamanism, Spiritualism, Santeria, Wicca, Voodoo, Palo Mayombe, Worship of dead, Divination, Spirit guides, Familiar spirits, Sorcery, Tarot cards, horoscopes and astrology, Charms and Crystals, Indian witchcraft, and Ouija boards.

- **Idolatry/False gods-** Work, Carer, Social media, Self-importance, People, Material things, Money, Sports, Business, Lifestyle, and all forms of entertainments such as television and movies. Please do not get me wrong all of these are good but the becomes bad if the take the place of God in your lives. What take a lot of your time outside God becomes your idols.
- **Bondage-** Hopelessness, Depression, Worry, Sorrow, Nervousness, Childlessness, Self-pity, Despair, Wars, greed, corruption, Pressure, Deception, Sadness, grief, Heaviness, Overbearing, hyperactivity, and blocked emotion.
- **Fear of-** Death, Accidents, Future, Disapproval, Confrontation, Rejection, Darkness, Loneliness, Trust, Love, Commitment, Animals, Germs, Sickness, Satan, and Panic attacks.
- **Pride-** Haughtiness, Ego, Intellectualism, Vanity, Self-righteousness, Spiritual pride, and ignorance.
- **Poverty -** Financial bondage, financial blockage, and financial destruction.
- **Perversion-** Lust, homosexuality, Masturbation, Adultery, Incest, Molestation of children, Rape, Bestiality, Harlotry, succubus, and Pornography.
- **Self-** Selfishness, Self-gratification, Self-will, Self-righteousness, Strife, Conflict, Bickering, Argumentative, Quarrelling, Fighting, Criticism, Judgemental, Gossiping, Finding fault, Accusations, offences, and Slanders.
- **Religion-** False doctrines, rituals, yoga, freemasonry, a tradition of men, Martial arts, Legalism, and all forms of other religions of the world which do not acknowledge Jesus Christ and the holy spirit as God's.
- **Antichrist-** False teachers and Prophets, False messiahs, Rebellion, Stubbornness, and all forms of unbelieve.
- **Bitterness-** Hatred, jealousy and Envy, revenge, resentment, lack of Forgiveness, Murder, Retaliation, Self-hate and doubt-both self and others.
- **Anger-** Rage, Temper, Wrath, Violence, Harassment, nightmares,
- **Mental illnesses-** Schizophrenia, Insomnia, Paranoia, distress, anxiety, depression, Retardation and Bipolar disorder. (Ramirez 2017).

With all these now in mind, you will admit that Satan is a real threat not only to your future vision and mission but also to your very existence here on earth. From the list above you will admit that there is already an area, if not areas in your life where Satan is the master with your full knowledge or without your full knowledge. The above areas are what Paul referred to as fiery darts of the wicked ones, which

Satan used to destroy our God-given destinies. If he cannot destroy us through the above devices, then he is able to keep us miserable and unproductive to our families and our communities. There are in the list above some of the Satanic devices that you would not believe comes from Satan to destroy us. But what does the Bible say the thief comes to steal, kill, and destroy. The reason why he is a thief is that if you were aware that he is using one of the devices above to destabilise you then you will never let him do it. That is why this book is important for you, to wake you up to this reality. The only way you can free yourselves from the above fiery darts is to accept Jesus Christ as your personal saviour.

Individual

It does not matter where you are, what you do or the power you think you have, Satan is after you and he can overpower you without God's protection. The best card he can play against you is to make sure that you cannot recognise whether he exists and can do you harm. It is important to make this observation that demons are not random in their attack on individuals, there must be a legal door or doors that you have opened for them to enter you. When you are born God assigned you a protective angel to guide and to protect you against the demons, but when you break out of God's protection zone you are prey to the demonic attacks. Demons look for open doors such as direct wilful sin, occult practice, generational curses, false religions, cursed objectives, cursed buildings, drug addictions, Ungodly soul ties, fears, unforgiveness, and abuses. Although we will not discuss each of these issues in details, all of these are devil door openers into the demonic kingdom. These are all baiting for Satan to get to you, and you must assess whether you are already involved in any of these practices.

The door openers mentioned above are used by his captives (human agents), the magicians, sorcerers, witches, diviners, astrologists, tarot card readers, and mediums to lure you into the demonic kingdom using these deadly baits. Once you are in, it is very hard to get out. In today's world, you will see many people being captives of the devil through drug abuse, alcohol, bitterness, arrogance, sexual immorality, hopelessness, depression, discouragement, and low self-esteem which they can find difficult to recover from.

There is No Crazy Human Being, but Rather the One Being Confused by the Thoughts of God and Satan in His Mind

We have discussed the human body as the battlefield in which the war between good and evil takes place. But we must also know exactly what area of your body is the target first before the battle spreads to the rest of your body. A human being's body is divided into the body (including all five senses), soul (mind, will and emotions), and spirit (the unseen and untouched being that communicates with God).

Human Soul as the Target

When God created human beings, he had given them a good, yet potentially dangerous thing – the human soul. Your soul is the steering wheel for your body. God gave each of us a soul (mind, will and emotions), to make our own decisions, but in close contact, coordination, and consultation with him. Our souls are where our decisions, creativities, imaginations, desires, and feelings are determined or directed. All that we do whether good or bad comes from our souls. Our bodies and our spirits are dictated and directed by our souls.

Satan Targets Your Soul by Bombarding Your Mind with His Thoughts

For Satan to destroy you he must first get hold of your soul. By getting hold of your soul, he is getting hold of your thoughts, desires, creativities, and feelings in order to control you easily. When this is done then everything else about you falls in place for him. He can now dictate what you do through your soul. This will come as a surprise to many people who think that their decisions are made without external forces interference. Well, if this is you then think again. Before I go into details about this let me ask you these questions; how many decisions have you made, which you have later regret? How many fights have you fought which you should not have fought? How many lies have you labelled against other people, which you should not have? How many people have you accused falsely, whom you should not have accused? How many rude words have you spoken against other people that you should not have spoken?

Well, it will depend on how honestly you can answer the above questions, but one thing is crystal clear from the above questions, all of them are bad. Yet we do not take notice of them daily when we direct them against other people. The questions above indicate that our important decision-making mechanism (the soul) is infiltrated and influenced by the demonic kingdom daily, making us look bad always in the eyes of others. Once Satan has controlled your thoughts, he can control your life. In real life, you begin to make decisions that are of no value or of little success. You are trapped and destined for hell.

How Can Satan Put Thoughts into Our Minds?

Satan uses our five senses (sound, smell, taste, sight, and touch) to put thoughts into our minds that become part of our decision-making mechanism. The way we communicate and detect information from the outside world determines how we make decisions sometimes in our lives. The information we receive from the five senses freaks us out if they are bad or bad news. Satan makes sure he brings bad news to us almost every day which can be in the form of doctors' reports of terminal sickness in our bodies, loss of a job, death of important family members, natural disasters, wars, and so forth. With the intensity of all this bad news on us, we can sometimes feel pressured to make bad decisions we later regret in life. But not only can this bad news alter our mental stability, but the also caused short term fear, stress, and disappointment. When we make decisions under fear, doubt, bitterness, and disappointment it is no longer us making decisions for ourselves but someone else making decisions on our behalves – who is Satan himself. Very frightening indeed, but a reality!!!

Interestingly as you can see, what we receive into our spirits from the outside world determines the decisions we make in life. For example, if we want to be intelligent, then we must read the books written by many great writers. If we are to be good future leaders then we must imitate our current charismatic leaders. So, the outside world is part of our internal world that determines the decisions we make in life, and Satan can infiltrate and heavily use these against us, and we must take notice of it.

No one was a victim of this deception more than King David; Satan knew that king David loved God and that David would never take any chances to compromise that, so Satan had to make sure that he infiltrated David's decision-making process by allowing the census to be conducted by his commander in chief of the armies of Israel-Joab. David had to do this without instruction from God. David thought he was the one making the decision, without realising that it was Satan. One may ask what is wrong with conducting the census? In the natural setting, there was nothing wrong with counting the number of soldiers and the people, to make a budget and future resources allocation for them. There was nothing wrong in the natural but there was something wrong in the spiritual realm. Even though David thought he was the one making the decision, God knew it was Satan. David's decision angered God: because first, he was not consulted by David for the decision-making process and second, David had put his trust in the number of soldiers of the armies of Israel but not God for his battles. As a result, David was punished by God.

Sometimes we think our enemies are the only sources Satan can use to get to us, but not our friends. This thinking is wrong and dangerous. For instance, the closest person Satan had to use to get to Jesus was his friend Simon Peter whose thoughts were influenced by Satan to deny Jesus Christ three times in the shortest possible moment. Furthermore, Judas Iscariot had to conceive wrong Satanic influenced thoughts in his mind to betray our Lord Jesus Christ and get him crucified. Simon Peter, in his natural mind as a close friend of Jesus Christ could not have conceived of denying his close friend three times, but little did he know that Satan could infiltrate his thoughts to make a bad decision in rejection of Jesus Christ as his close friend.

Once Satan has controlled all the vital organs in the soul, he makes sure that he develops mental strongholds within our brains that cannot easily be altered by new alternative information that comes to our ways – particularly those thoughts that are from God. He must make sure that he blinds your five senses in your body and the spirit from within you that is receptive to God's information. In many cases in the natural world, we begin to develop instincts within our mindset that reject the truth. Especially the truth that will get us into trouble now or in the future by developing these strongholds; always making excuses for the bad decisions we make, instead of accepting the mistakes. The denial of truth, taking our frustration out on others who are not part of our problems, and compromising our beliefs systems for others who we think can be offended by us. These mental strongholds become the basis on which Satan operates through us.

Families

Just as you are the target, your family is also the target. Why is this? Because family is the union of man and woman that bring forth future generations of children that will destroy the agenda of Satan on earth. But not only is the family, a unit in which children are born into, but it is also the unit in which God blesses individuals, communities, societies, and nations. The only way Satan can control the world (which is his wish), is to put a brake on family production (future generations of children) and influence the one he has (the current generation) to have a family of rebels, who reject God on earth. Many families do not realise this early enough in their marriage, that there is an enemy after them, not only to destroy their current union but future unions of their children following. It is in the interest of every family to raise, mould, shape, and direct their children in a God-fearing and loving way, but Satan wants to make sure that this does not happen – by getting children to rebel against parents, and husband and wife to break up in their marriage. The cycle repeats itself. If you cannot raise your children in God-loving ways, it is an assurance that your children will not raise their children in a God-loving and caring way. The family unit in which God blesses the entire generations is broken down, missing God's blessings through rebellion and destabilisation by Satan. For instance, we know that King David was a God loving man in his walk with the Lord, and because of this, his children in the generation following were also blessed. We could see this later when some of David's children (Solomon and Rehoboam and many others) sinned against God, he could not destroy them because of their father's blessings upon their lives.

When God blessed the family, he blessed even the generation following. As a matter of fact, nothing Satan fears the most than the family whose many generations are blessed by God. We could see this from **Genesis 6**, when God had blessed all living things on earth including mankind, and particularly Noah, to be the future family from which the whole earth would be blessed. To poison the future generations of mankind on earth, to rebel against God, he had to send his angels to enter one of his sons –Ham, who got cursed by his father because while drunk he laughed at his nakedness. Satan had to produced demonic rebels against God on the earth immediately after the flood. Noah being holy in his generation was spared by God to be the source of the family unit from which the future generation of mankind was blessed, yet Satan had to sabotage the blessings of God over the descendants of humanity.

Now it came to pass when men began to multiply on the face of the earth, and daughters were born to them, that the sons of God saw the daughters of men, that they were beautiful, and they took wives for themselves of all whom they chose. And the Lord said, "My Spirit shall not strive with man forever, for he is indeed flesh; yet his days shall be one hundred and twenty years. "There were giants on the earth in those days, and also afterwards, when the sons of God came into the daughters of men and they bore children to them. Those were the mighty men who were of old, men of renown. Then the Lord saw that the wickedness of man was great in the earth and that every intent of the thoughts of his heart was only evil continually. And the LORD was sorry that He had made man on the earth, and He was grieved in His heart. So the Lord said, "I will destroy man whom I have created from the face of the earth, both man and beast, creeping thing and birds of the air, for I am sorry that I have made them". But Noah found grace in the eyes of the Lord. (Genesis 6:1-8). NKJV.

In the world today the family unit is under serious attack from the devil, by distorting marriages. People today, instead of having their marriages in the churches, choose to have them officiated by their own friends and relatives, who conduct their marriages vows at beaches and parks. Very often it used to be the work of God-fearing religious leaders at churches. Instead of having their marriages being officiated in the churches by God-fearing religious leaders who could read for them the vows that enable God's blessings over their marriage, it is seen as a waste of time. Furthermore, through abortion, the devil is eliminating future generations of children who could serve God and be blessings to their families. Let me be clear, the killing of unborn children is a crime against God. There are no Godly blessings upon those parents who kill their children through abortion. Besides, the quest for the destruction of families, people under the influence of Satan have resorted to marrying man-to-man, and woman-to-woman and these unions cannot produce future generations of children on earth. The introduction of contraceptives is an attempt to reduce future generations of people through which God can continue to bless the human family or society. It is not about genuine and honest birth control, as doctors and politicians plus other interest groups have made you to be believed. The voices in support of family units are growing quieter and quieter every day in the world because there is a justification of sins. People who condemn these acts have been labelled as bigots and out of touch with the world by people who have little or no knowledge at all about the driver behind these things-who is Satan. It is

Satan's wish that the number of rebels against God increases day by day on earth, for him to take over the earth.

Churches

It must be made clear that God is a God of order. He established heavens and earth through his words. As a matter of fact, everything he has created operates through his laws and orders. When he had created everything, he brought all things under his word (Jesus Christ), in whom everything was created and was established. Jesus Christ is the head of the church just as the man is the head of the family in the ideal family unit. The Church is the united body of believers who believes in the Son of God. The church is a place in which Christians gather to praise and worship God, which Satan hates the most. In fact, what got him into trouble in heaven was the fact that he wanted to be like God – to be praised and worshipped. He attacks the church to disperse people who worship God so that no one calls on God's name on earth. He does this through false religions, legalism, division, confusion, violence, sexual abuse of vulnerable groups, doubt, unbelief, wrong perceptions, and denominationalism.

There is one thing that Satan knows that people of God do not know, and that is the fact that God does not like disunity, and he cannot bless a chaotic and dysfunctional church. For people of God to experience God's blessings and power in the church they must be united, and in humility with the authentic love of each other, that pleases God. The biggest deception we witness today is the fact that many Christians believe too much in their denominations and their doctrines that discriminate against the other people of God. We have seen today for example, in many denominations, people turn to discriminate Christians based on the baptism by immersion or sprinkling of water and the doctrines of the church. Either way, many people are turned away from churches because the kind of baptism is not supported by the doctrines of their churches. It is not meant to be that way because God does not discriminate.

Above all else, we are blessed in churches, not on the doctrines and laws established by humans but our allegiances to Christ as the head of the church. We may have different rules and regulations, ways of worship, teachings, and dancing styles but united by the name and blood of Jesus Christ as the head of the church. To lessen the advancement of the kingdom on earth Satan makes sure that he divides the people along the ethnic lines, class, race, personality, and gender to cause confusion for people of God to be less effective in their work for God.

Societies

Nothing is more vulnerable to demonic attack today than human society. The main institutions of human society today such as politics, business and communities have come under distortion by Satan to the extent that they no longer have common beliefs, norms, values, and creeds shared by them. In politics, there is no longer care for common citizens but care for one's own interest in the form of corruption and greed that has plagued many governments around the world today. Many politicians today have come out openly in support of same-sex marriage instead of the ideal family unit characterised by husband, wife, and their children. Many societies have rejected Christianity as a true religion and Jesus Christ as the head because they think it is dominated by certain human races and originated from certain human societies. In business corrupt dealings and contracts have been signed, which have exploited the ordinary citizens in favour of politicians, leaving a certain section of the society poor and in poverty forever. In today's human societies many people have an advantage over their other fellow human beings because they have looked after their interests above that one of their neighbours – a case which is against God's will for their neighbours.

In the history of the world, we have seen a rise in governments that support the superiority of their fellow human beings in that part of the world over other people in other parts of the world. For example, we have seen the rise and fall of radical governments led by radical people like Idi Amin of Ugandan, Adolf Hitler of Germany, Mussolini of Italy, Jong-Un of north -Korea and countless of other world leaders that have killed and continued to oppress human beings today based on their demonically influenced ideologies. Without a doubt, many of these people were provoked, stirred up, empowered, and enabled by Satan to destroy entire nations and certain groups of people to establish permanent hatred between people.

When sin entered the world, it did not corrupt humans alone but the institutions of God's blessings. To increase his number of rebels Satan makes sure that he destabilises individuals, families, churches, and societies so they miss God's blessings. Whether it is slavery, human trafficking, wars, chemical weapons, and wage theft, all are designed to oppress our fellow human beings through wicked people that think only about themselves. With this mindset, it seems that human society is long gone as there are no collectives and common views about the world we live in today. What is wrong is no longer collectively condemned by societies as they did against apartheid rule in South Africa and the killing of Jews in Adolf Hitler's, Germany. As of today, human societies are badly divided and with no future direction because they have rejected God.

The Devil's Strategies for the Battle

Benjamin Franklin once said, he who does not plan, has already planned to fail. I wonder where the people got this saying from if indeed it is not from the spiritual world. God is a God of order and planning, and so is Satan. The reason why St. Paul compared spiritual warfare with physical warfare, which is the fact that there must be a plan in place for it to be fought and won. There must not be only weapons, bullets and people involved in the war, but tactics, ways, tricks, strategies, and an overall plan for the battle to be won by either side of the parties involved. But note this, it is common-sense that everyone plans for war, but the victorious party is the one that has a better plan and strategy in place. In any case, the war is never won by anybody who has a gun, bullets, and pulls a trigger against his opponent, but rather by anybody who has tricks, tactics, plans and strategies in place for the battle. Neither is the battle won by anybody who has both enough human resources and material resources but with no proper plan in place for the battle.

One thing must be made absolutely clear, to all Christians, Satan has a better plan and strategy in place to fight you then you do. How do I know that Satan has a better plan than you? Well, the bible tells us that he is wiser than Daniel, one of the greatest men who had ever lived and who had better plan and strategies against his enemies in the like of King Nebuchadnezzar of Babylon. The main overall plan for Satan against you is to cause you to doubt, question and reject God. And if you are wiser enough to accept that there is God, then he will make sure that he manipulates your mind by attacking it with different thoughts in order to distort that truth in your mind.

What he did in the garden of Eden to Adam and Eve is what he continues to do today. He got Adam and Eve to not appreciate what God had already done for them, by allowing them to enjoy everything good about his creation (knowledge of good things given to them), except the knowledge of one bad thing God did not want them to know (knowledge of evil), Satan who was present at the garden, which they were so determined to know. This is exactly what he wants you to do; complain about things you do not have so that you cannot be appreciative of what God has already done for you. One thing that will make you lose your life, is what Satan is after in your life. No matter what, there is always one thing that you will want to have that you do not have – it may be money, spouse, power, pride, honour and glory, strength, wisdom and so much more, that will cause God to curse you if you are to acquire in a wrong way.

The one rule of thumb you must remember is that Satan wants to pull you away from the goodness of God, because he knows he cannot defeat you in the presence of God and with God's protective hedges around you. He wants you to disown God so that you can join him in rebellions against God. This is all done through deception. Among the top priorities in his deceptions list is that if he can get you to doubt or reject Jesus Christ and the bible as the true source of the truth for your life, then he is a winner. The reason he operates in deceptions is that he knows that you will quickly discover his tricks if he does them openly and in a straightforward way. In fact, he is a chameleon that does not want you to know him as the true thief, killer, and destroyer of human beings. He has nothing good in him except what the bible tells us here; **"The thief does not come except to steal, and to kill, and to destroy. (John 10:10). NKJV.**

Satan has among others these four distinctive strategies he uses to deceive people and particularly Christians, as namely, desires, deception, disobedience, and death.

Desires

It must first be noticed that the word desire is not a bad word, but its miss-use is the problem. When God created humans, he wanted them to have what they want from him in the forms of desires. What we want is what we call desire. It is not bad to plan to succeed and to commit yourself to the causes of your life. But this is where we go wrong; our desires must be within our time frame, resources, and energy and above all be legitimate and justifiable before God. If our desires are not within these limits and not justifiable before God, then they become illegitimate and sinful in nature, bringing curses over our lives. In other words when our desires become uncontrollable, then Satan can get us to commit sin. What is uncontrollable in our lives is what gets us into problems with God. If we are after something that becomes so much greater than our legitimate ways of getting it, then it has the potential to get us to sin. This is very important to note.

So, what does Satan do? He gets us to overplay our hands beyond our legitimate desires. For example, it is good to have a business; but it is not good to overcharge customers. It is good to eat food, but it is not good to overeat. It is good to sleep, but it is not good to oversleep. It is good to have wealth, but it is not good to acquire it through corruption. It is good to have sex, but it is not good to commit adultery. It is good to disagree, but it is not good to quarrel and fight. Can I ask you this question; what have you noticed here? All legitimate desires given to us by God can become sins if we overuse them or if we are committed to getting them wrongly. Satan overplays these legitimate rights of the desires given to you by God to the extent that he wants you to believe that you can never do without them. So be warned; the part of your life that is out of control is what will get God to reject you if you continue in defiance and without repentance. This is what gets us into temptation. Apostle James put this even better; **Let no one say when he is tempted, "I am tempted by God"; for God cannot be tempted by evil, nor does He Himself tempt anyone. But each one is tempted when he is drawn away by his own desires and enticed. Then, when desire has conceived, it gives birth to sin; and sin, when it is full-grown, brings forth death. James 1:13-14. NKJV.**

So, let me be clear here, the main problem for you here is not even the devil or God but your own desires. Before the devil comes in, you will acknowledge that there is part of your life that must be out of control to warrant the devil to come and tempt you. It may sometimes not be you who has committed the sins, but somebody in your life either your father, mother, siblings, and relatives. Even though Satan has power, it is a limited power that he uses against a person who has a broken relationship with God, particularly those who have violated God laws. For example, St-Paul had God's call over his life, but God had no problem with him until he overused his Satan given and influenced power against God's peoples. Satan had to make sure without or with Paul's knowledge, that he developed a zeal against God people by not only killing them but also bragging about it openly to his colleagues – the Pharisees. Remember, God cannot be mocked and so he had to act, or else Christians would have quit believing in the God who can save them against evil. So, everything must not start and end with Satan, check yourself first. Check your roots first. Has anyone in your lineage been a worshipper of the devil? God is a just God, and he cannot allow Satan into your life unless there is something to be corrected.

Deception

The main reason why Satan cannot operate openly is that he will get no one if people realise, he is the one influencing communities, societies, churches, hospitals, governments, businesses, and schools. So, what does he do? He goes to our churches, schools, hospitals, communities, and governments through us (the people) with or without our full knowledge. You see our instinct tells us that he does exist without us paying attention to what we are saying about him. Isn't it acknowledging his existence when we say things such as you are a devil, or he is a devil; that is magic or you need magic to win; my life is a hell on earth; I will ask God to take my life (yet you do not acknowledge it is not God who kills you but Satan); and all forms of swearing you made not to do evil. So, we do acknowledge there is a devil, but we do not know the magnitudes of his threats to our lives.

Deception is when someone else manipulates the truth in his favour, not your favour. Obviously, because he is far too intelligent than human beings, he will complicate these deceptions, tricks, and techniques to the extent that you will never know them as false or deceptions. He does not give you straightforward lies, but half-truth and half-lie information. It is common-sense that a lie is a lie, so why should he lie to you openly? There is one area in our lives that has been paid little or no attention at all – the thoughts in our minds. Have you ever questioned where the thoughts in your mind come from? Well, although most of them can be ours, many of them also, I must tell you today, come from God or Satan. What Satan does is to put wrong thoughts into our minds that we think are ours yet are from the devil – particularly the negative thoughts. Again, let us go by our rule of thumb; half-truth and half-lie thoughts that he put into our minds. For example, St. Paul was committed to killing Christians, not because he wanted to, but to please his Jewish colleagues (the Pharisees), who saw Christianity as a threat to their culture and their religion – Judaism. Behind this action by Paul, was the devil who hated the spread of Christianity because it was the real threat to his kingdom. If it was not the devil behind it, then how can somebody in his right mind brag about the killings of his fellow human beings? But little did he know that he was overplaying his hands against God.

Surprisingly, what many Christians do not know is the fact that Satan does not get to you through an unbaited hook, nor does he openly advertise that 'I am the devil and I want to attack you. He does it in a smarter way than you think. He comes in with small bad things or your daily bad habits you are involved in. For example, the little drinks we take every day that ends up being giants in our lives in form of addiction that resulted into heavy drunkenness, leading to family fights, children drunkenness, poverty, and finally death. Furthermore, he can also come to you in a form of a rude conversation that you should not have had, a little pen you should not have taken away at your workplace, a demonically influenced movie you should not have watched, and a relationship you should not have had in the first place. Everything starts nice and in small portions of your life until it can grow into a big giant in your life that is out of control. No better analogy I can use here than the analogy of a fisherman and his hook. The fisherman knows that he cannot catch fish by just putting his hook into the water without worms or meat, because he knows nothing will attract fish to the plain mental hook. He knows very well that what will attract fish is the meat or worms which is desired by fish as food. The sources of food for fish becomes a deadly trap for fish. This is exactly what Satan does to us; he baits us through those things that we love that become our deadly trap by him.

Disobedience

What gets us into trouble with God is our disobedience against him. That assignment from God you refused to do in the church, that warning you refused to heed from your parents, and that action you know is bad and you still do. One reason among others that God gave us the written word (the bible), is to let us avoid all the things that are not good for us. When we do those things that God told us not to do in his constitution (bible), then we rebel against him. When Adam and Eve disobeyed God, by not respecting his instructions, and ate from the tree of knowledge of good and evil, it was a direct rebellion against God resulting in their death. This is also true today for us as we continue to do those things that we have been warned in the bible as bad, yet we continue to commit them even after we are warned, which will result in our rebellion against God, leading to our death. Satan is the number one master of disobedience against God, and he knows how to play this game the best in your life so that God can reject you.

The greatest master of rebellion against God was Jonah in the bible, who refused to go on God's assignment to the people of Nineveh, in order to go and warned them to leave their bad ways (shedding of blood, daylight robbery, raping, corruption, and worshipping of idols) and return to God. Jonah had to put his own interests above that of God, first; by putting his security above the powers of God. He doubted whether God would really protect him in that highly populated city, not to be killed by them. While delivering that important message. Second, he did not want God to forgive the people of Nineveh because they were enemies of Jews–his people. He wanted his hatred for the people of Nineveh to be an opportunity in which God would destroy them. There are many cases in the bible where people rebelled against God that ended up as a disaster upon them. The reason why we have too many problems today in our lives is that we have rejected God's calls on our lives. We continue to behave as if we are the creators of ourselves.

Death

To the right is the circle of the deadly sins we must avoid if we are to be friends with God. These things kill us before we physically disappear from the earth. When we do these things, we are spiritually dead, before we are physically dead. This is exactly what happened to Adam and Eve in the garden of Eden. They were dead spiritually before they had to die physically. Just as Adam and Eve were spiritually dead before they were physically dead, we are dead today spiritually before we are dead physically, if we do not acknowledge that we have sinned and repent of that sin before God.

Death is perhaps the strongest weapon Satan continues to unleash against us, as Christians. Even though Christ died for us, we continue to fear death. But not only that Satan has lied to us that when we talk about death, we will also probably die prematurely. We are fearful about the physical disappearance of our bodies on earth, but less fearful about our true selves; our souls and spirits being put into eternal condemnation afterwards by God. The bible warns us not to fear those who kill our bodies but rather the one who puts souls into hell, ***"and do not fear those who kill the body but cannot kill the soul. But rather fear Him who is able to destroy both soul and body in hell. (Matthew 10:28). NKJV.***

The deception by the devil is that he wants you to believe that your true you is the body and not your soul and spirit. What he does not want you to know is that your true you do not die when your body dies. The benefits of this book among others is to let you know your true self is not your body but your soul and spirit, which are eternal. Your soul and spirit do not die once your body dies physically;

Source: Prince, 2015, https://faceforwardcolumbus.com

your soul and spirit go and either live in hell with Satan or in heaven with God. Once you know this, then Satan will always be a loser against you. Why will he waste his time killing what he will never benefit from? But this is not enough to stop the devil from attacking you. Once he knows that you know this, then he can attempt to frustrate your life here on earth through his other devices such as fear, doubt, and rejection.

When we break our fellowship with God, we can become ineffective and powerless Christians who can do nothing in this life. This is the reality today that Satan has lied to many people to believe that when they become God's ministers, they will be poor and that they will never have the freedom they need to enjoy their beautiful lives on earth. The lie is so pervasive that some Pastors today believe that they can preach God's gospel that has nothing to benefit them. The idea that you can be poor while serving the rich God is incomprehensible for me. This is totally wrong, as the bible tells us that we must eat from the gospel if we are gospel ministers, **"Even so the Lord has commanded that those who preach the gospel should live from the gospel" (1 Corinthians 9:14).** This was not the case with the tribe of Levi, who were never given land according to God's instructions but lived off the tithes and offerings given to God by the people of Israel. So where does this assertion that we can be poor while serving rich God come from? If indeed is it not Satan's lying to us. You must work and God will bless the work of your hands. We carry God blessings if we walk in his ways and he will bless what we do if we work.

Sometimes we think that death is when we physically disappear away from the earth. I want to tell you that is always not the case. The actual death is when a person is still alive physically but dead spiritually. To put it in context; our bodies do not communicate with God, but our spirits do while we are still alive. So, when our spirits do not relate or communicate with the spirit of God, while we are still alive then we are dead spiritually before we are dead physically. Adam and Eve were declared dead by God as soon as they ate from the tree of knowledge of good and evil before they physically disappeared from the earth. At times we use this phrase against our opponents; "dead man walking." This phrase means that a man is dead when he has no tangible plans for his life in the forms of vision and mission, career, virtue, relationship and values and norms to live for. Sometimes a meaningless life without direction leads to stress, depression, and finally suicidal thoughts leading to death if they are not controlled early enough. As a matter of fact, we often question God or even blame him when we lead miserable lives that hit a dead-end. We begin to have low opinions about God's intention for our lives, creating doubt and unbelief in our minds about God's genuineness to help us at the difficult moments of our lives. We become double-minded and receive nothing from God. Very deadly indeed.

Chapter 2

Confession, Repentance and Baptism of The Holy Spirit

Confession
" Sin"

Sin came into the world because of Luciferic rebellion and his poisoning of humanity's mind to rebel against God, and to that effect, the earth was cursed, and humans were also cursed. As a matter of fact, these curses are still relevant and are experienced today by people; a woman continues to give birth in unimaginable pain and a man continues to till the ground very hard in order to have his meal. The whole earth with her living and nonliving things continue to live under the curse of Adam and his wife Eve.

There is nothing God hates like Satan, who had caused mankind to sin against him. It must be known that those who worship Satan are subject to God's wrath and judgement as they are enemies of God. When God's anger is aroused from heaven, he comes to Satanic strongholds with a full force in the forms of; whirlwind, flood, fire, thunderstorm, lightning flashes, trumpet, volcanic eruptions to destroy them. It must be made clear that those people who have joined Satan in their rebellion against God are doom and destine for hell, where their soul will tormented and burned forever in the unquenchable fire. Sin is a precursor to human destruction. Committing sin without repentance is rejecting God's presence in your life. This allows automatic devil dominant in your life. Sin is what the devil feeds on.

God's blessing is contingent upon not worshipping Satan. Many people of the world are deceived today to believe that when they are doing well in areas such as stable family, finances, health, favour and power and authority, they think it is a blessing from God. Let me tell you this it is not always necessarily the case. God cannot bless sinful human beings. This is the biggest blind spot for many Christians and non-Christians alike. Today, and as it has always been, the wealth of the world can be gotten in three ways: first, yes indeed from God if someone is a committed Christian who loves and follows his laws; second, through individual hard work because of their will to succeed; third, from Satan in form of corrupted ways such as greed in business through corrupt deals and contracts, corruption in politics, robbery, drug-dealings and so much more. What does this tell you? It is telling you that most of the wealth today in the world does not come from God as it is obtained through corruption, greed, illegal drug dealings, robbery, and corruption in politics. This wealth has no God blessing and has nothing to do with God. It is also important to note that even those who have gotten their wealth from their hard work, have no God blessing because they have not invited God into their affairs. The bible puts it very clear that if you have disconnected your soul, spirit, and body from God, he considers that still as idolatry. If you want your wealth to be enjoyed by many generations of your family members no matter what ways you got it, you must repent and seek God's blessings for it. There is nothing God loves like a person who acknowledges his or her sins, repents, and turns away from them.

Satan's strategy is to get you to rebel against God to own you. Obviously, God hates sin, and he will have nothing to do with a person who likes sin. God will remove his protective hedges over your life. When this happens then you are done- Satan can mess around with you the way he wants. What the devil owns will be destroyed through sickness, disease, poverty, and tragedy. This is very important to note for those who think worshipping Satan is something pleasing and with no consequences from him. Besides, rebellion against God is in the form of sin committed by you, former iniquity (sins of your ancestors) and transgression (complete rejection of God by you), that enables you to miss God's blessings over your life. Furthermore, he gets you to disobey God's laws, judgement, statutes, and commandments. Pay attention to this: Satan is a persecutor who builds a lawsuit against you if he is to own you and to larger extent your other family members before God in the court of heaven. He makes sure he owns you, your family, your community, and your society permanently, through the sense of entitlement (he enters a covenant with these groups of people).

He does it in the following ways: Firstly, through sin, Sins are those immoral acts such as hatred, jealousy, covetousness, adultery, stealing, greed, fornication, homosexuality, drunkenness and so much more that you commit against another person. You must avoid these traps of Satan by all means. Before you do anything wrong consider whether it is legal, conscientious, ethical and does it affect somebody else in a negative way, in order to avoid these traps of the devil.

Secondly, through iniquity. This involves covenants (sacrifice through the shedding of blood), dedications (where children are given to the devil as his own), trades (where the family gives material resources or human resources in exchange for Satanic security and protection), and rebellion (where people of certain families reject God's ways and laws). Most importantly, "generational curse; this is one of the ways Satan blocks blessings from God. A generational curse is a sin passed down from one generation to the next generation of the same family lineage or bloodline. It happened when one member or members of the same family lineage or bloodline made a covenant with Satan. The covenant is made with the sacrifice of an animal or human being to Satan, to secure his provisions in the form of resources, security, authority, and power. Once this is done it is binding on the parties involved, which is unbreakable for generations following the first generation that made that covenant. In these families, it is Satan who has complete responsibility to bless and to punish every single member of the family who is involved and entitled to the covenant. In blessing, Satan can secure family resources and security of every single member of the family involved in the covenant. In punishing he kills without consequences from God, any family members who are involved directly or directly in the covenant. You will observe that family members die prematurely, die with the same disease, children die at birth, and poverty recurs and so much more in those families. For the member and members of that family to be free, the curse must be broken in the court of heaven. To stop this legal right of Satan from your family lineage, one person who is a strong believer in God must use the blood of

Jesus Christ to clear the family name from the court of heaven. The people from the family lineage must live a Christian life that is free of sins. This means they must acknowledge their wrongdoings to God, for God to forgive them.

Thirdly, through a transgression, this is where individuals, community and society reject God completely. They do not respect God's laws, judgement, and commandments. People in your family or ancestry would have made covenants with the devil to secure demonic powers, protection, provisions, and empowerment and they will have nothing to do with God. This has been true and continues to be up to today in every culture and every race of people on different continents. For example, people who are sick today face difficulty to be healed even if they are Christians because someone else on their behalf would have entitled them to the demonic powers as their own. The rights of these demons must be revoked at the court of heaven so that people are free from illnesses.

Unless these sins, transgressions and iniquities are dealt with, individual, community and society will never experience God's blessings. The only way you can live a free life in this world is to confess that you have sinned directly or indirectly against God by committing one of the above sins or committing all the above sins. Sometimes it may not be you who has committed these sins but maybe your parents who have made a covenant with the devil, that entitled him to have generational claims of you through your parent's bloodline. Whether it is either you or your parents, you must admit that you have sinned against God through confession. Please note God's blessing is not about having large sums of money, a wife, a husband, and children, power and authority, and business, as many people are made to believe it is much bigger than all of these. People have had these things and they are still in problems. God's blessing, therefore, is about having a long life, having guaranteed safety when we walk on his ways, peace, love, and joy to be able to enjoy the fruits of your hard work.

Repentance

The only way to come out of these curses is to accept Jesus Christ as your personal saviour, who died for you to have peace with God. All the diseases and other forms of human sufferings are connected to the curses of Adam and Eve, which we are born into. God is waiting for you to move away from the kingdom of darkness (Satan) into the kingdom of God (Jesus Christ). Unless you do so you will continue to remain in the curse. True repentance means admitting that you have sinned against God and you are willing to completely turn away from your sins. By doing so you are changing your mind and your heart for good never to think about them anymore. The only way you can have eternal salvation is to have true repentance from your heart and mind.

"Truly, these times of ignorance God overlooked, but now commands all men everywhere to repent" (Acts 17:30).

"Repent therefore and be converted, that your sins may be blotted out, so that times of refreshing may come from the presence of the Lord" (Acts 3:19).

"I tell you, no; but unless you repent you will all likewise perish" (Luke 13:5).

"Those who are well don't need a physician, but those who are sick. I did not come to call the righteous, but sinners, to repentance" (Mark 2:17).

You cannot be defiance about sin and the need for repentance in order to have peace with God, but you must know this; it is also foolishness for you to come to this world and leave this world having not known how it came about, only for you to be told by God that you are going to hell. Because you did not bother to find God while you had a chance. Once you are dead, the responsibility as to where you will go does no longer rest with you. Pause about that a moment. Whether you oppose it or not, it does not change anything at all about heaven and hell. That is why the prophet Isaiah said, "Seek the Lord while He may be found, call upon Him while He is near. Let the wicked forsake his way, and the unrighteous man his thoughts; Let him return to the Lord and He will have mercy on him; and to our God, for He will abundantly pardon." ***(Isaiah 55:6-7)***. Repentance is the only way forward with God.

It must be made clear that God does not need your knowledge about him in order for you to repent. One of the reasons among others that we reject God is because we use our human logic to acknowledge his existence and to repent thereafter. We want to be sure that God exists before we repent, which is contrary to faith that is required of us by God to acknowledge his existence. Our human logic is of no help to God He did not give knowledge to you to help him but rather, to help yourself and your other fellow men. He provides you with knowledge, abilities, and skills to understand the hard things to help your fellow human beings. If you want to know things of God, you must shun your human wisdom. You must approach things of God through the position of need not the position of satisfaction. No PhD, master's degree and Degree will enable you to know things of God. God hates the proud and God only teaches the humble. So, let no one boast in himself or other men. If there were no challenges beyond humankind's wisdom, humankind would not need God at all. We do not like death, wars, diseases, poverty, natural disasters, pestilences, and yet all these deadly events happen against our will because we reject God. So, where is humanity's wisdom in solving all these things? The wisdom of men and women comes to nothing if tough situations hit them such as sicknesses (cancer, Aids, Ebola): natural disasters (hurricanes, tsunamis, earthquakes, volcanic eruptions, and storms), and all forms of accidents: planes, car, ships, and all forms of family difficulties: divorce, finances, and childlessness. You do not need to wait to be hit by one of the above disasters to know God. Before you become desperate and helpless in search of God at difficult moments of need, now is the time. Repent and turn to God for the salvation of your soul.

Note, God only shows up in the affairs of a person, when his or her wisdom is completely exhausted. You can be educated but still, live a miserable life if you are not with God. Here are the reasons why you need God throughout your life. He has held back his wisdom, courage, and understanding to be accessed only by those who wholeheartedly seek him and love him. That is why you can have your education but remain helpless without his wisdom to apply what you have learned daily, over difficult matters of your life. ***Isaiah 55:8-12*** says, "For My thoughts are not your thoughts, nor are your ways My ways," says the Lord. "For as the heavens are higher than the earth, so are My ways higher than your ways, and My thoughts than your thoughts. For as the rain comes down, and the snow from heaven, and do not return there, but water the earth, and make it bring forth and bud, that it may give seed to the sower and bread to the eater, so shall My word be that goes forth from My mouth; it shall not return to Me void, but it shall accomplish what I please, and it shall prosper in the thing for which I sent it. For you shall go out with joy and be led out with peace; the mountains and the hills shall break forth into singing before you, and all the trees of the field shall clap their hands. The mysteries of God kingdom simply beat mankind logic and wisdom.

Baptism of The Holy Spirit

Fact: God only created our spirits in his image and his likeness but not our bodies and souls. If you want to connect to God, then you must allow his spirit to operate in you and through you. It is only "the Holy Spirit" who will teach you deep things of God and you must seek him and keep him.

Although we are spirits as humankind, we have a body that hinders our spiritual eyes from seeing spiritual things or other spirits. Hence, the spirits do see us, but we do not see the spirits so long as we are in the body; it is only when we die and leave the body that our spirits will see other spirits including the spirit of God. The only way we can see spirits is through faith believing that spirits do exist including God, who is a spirit.

It is by faith believing that the spirits do exist, and they can communicate to us (humankind), that warrant the spirits to speak to us. The first spirit that would have an encounter with us, if we believed and were baptized by it, is the Holy Spirit of God. It is this spirit that connects us to the other spirits as namely, Jesus Christ and God almighty.

The Kingdom of God is Within You, The Holy Spirit

Without the Holy Spirit (God's Wisdom), **hu**mankind will have zero communication with God. If you do not have the spirit of God in you, you are not a child of God. Another hard fact. There is nothing in between, either you are with the devil or with God!!! Human beings have no middle line. Because there is something beyond the wisdom of humankind

It is through the Holy Spirit that we as Christians, are deeply grounded and rooted in the things of God. As with all the information from the kingdom, God flows through him to us. It is through Holy Spirit revelations to us that the true meaning of words of the bible can be understood. It is through the Holy Spirit that we become children of God. He is the Godhead's (God the Father, God the Son, and God the Holy Spirit), representative here on earth. The Holy Spirit is known by various names, including the "Spirit of God, the "Spirit of truth, and finger of God." His roles among the Christians are to; "comfort, convict, advocate, guide, counsel and help children of God over their daily challenges the devil present to them."

The verses below point to the fact that the Holy Spirit dwells in you and as a kingdom representative here on earth:

Luke 17:20-21 says, "Now when He was asked by the Pharisees when the kingdom of God would come, He answered them and said, 'The kingdom of God does not come with observation; nor will they say, 'See here!' or 'See there!' For indeed, the kingdom of God is within you."

Ephesians 4:30 says, "And do not grieve the Holy Spirit of God, with whom you were sealed for the day of redemption".

This practically means that the Holy Spirit can be annoyed, resisted, and disappointed by Christians because he is a person and has feelings. Pay attention to this: the new covenant under our Lord Jesus is unlike the old covenant of Moses which consisted of laws. Judgements and commandments of God were written on stone; now instead, the laws, judgements, and commandments of God are written in people's hearts and minds. It means that you and I are left with no excuse for later saying, "Oh Lord, I did not hear or know about the Kingdom". For example, in every language, in every tradition, in every culture no one can claim not to have heard or known God. Also, practically as persons, you wrestle daily between what is good and what is evil in your hearts and minds. For example, if you choose what is evil when you are aroused to anger, the Holy Spirit will convict you afterwards and you will come to the realisation that you have committed a crime. That is a work of the Holy Spirit practically in you. His job is to guide you away from sin but when you overruled him, he will, later on, convict you. So, he is your first protector before the army and police forces of your nations. He is also your judge before the judges of your nations. If you live respecting the voice of the Holy Spirit inside you, you will never commit any crime. When you commit a crime and repent of it when he convicts, you can ask him to go and represent you in the court of law as he will enable you to speak powerful words people will never admit that they are coming from you.

Jesus Christ, who was a hundred per cent human being became a hundred per cent God through his baptism with the Holy Spirit. It is important to note that the Holy Spirit descended on him in the form of a dove accompanying the voice saying, "You are my son in whom I am well pleased. He was the absolute power Jesus relied on to preach the gospel to the people, nations, and kingdoms of the world. **Luke 4:18** *"The Spirit of the Lord is upon Me because He has anointed me to preach the gospel to the poor; He has sent me to heal the broken-hearted, to proclaim liberty to the captives and recovery of sight to the blind, to set at liberty those who are oppressed".*

How Do You Allow the Holy Spirit to Operate Through You?

The Holy Spirit can be activated through a believer by prayer. ***Luke 11:13* says,** "*If you then, being evil, know how to give good gifts to your children, how much more will your heavenly Father give the Holy Spirit to those who ask Him!*" He can also be imparted to a believer through the laying of hands by a pastor who has the anointing of the Holy Spirit. Where the spirit of God is there is freedom, and through him, you are able to pray to God according to his will and it is also through him that you are able to forgive other people who have wronged you. It is through the power of the Holy Spirit that you are filled with hope if everything around you is against you and about to take you off. If the Holy Spirit is in you, you can be rarely sick, and if you are sick you will be healed. *1 Corinthians 6:19-20* says, "*Do you not know that your bodies are the temple of the Holy Spirit, who is in you, who you have received from God? You are not your own; you were bought at a price. therefore, honour God with your bodies*". It is when you are filled with the Holy Spirit that you can preach the gospel of Jesus Christ to the poor, captives, limbless, blind and the deaf. It is through the power of the Holy Spirit that you can cast out demons, heal the sick, speak in tongues, and hold serpents with your hands and they will not, by all means, harm you. *(Mark 16:15-18).*

How Do You Know Whether You Have the Holy Spirit?

Galatians 5:22-23- "But the fruit of the Spirit is love, joy, peace, longsuffering, kindness, goodness, faithfulness, gentleness, self-control. Against such, there is no law". When you have experienced these fruits in your life you will have unwavering hope in the things of God. And this hope does not put you into shame, as it has been poured into your hearts through the work of the Holy Spirit.

Jude 1:20-21 says, "But you, dear friends, by building yourselves up in your most holy faith and praying in the Holy Spirit, keep yourselves in God's love as you wait for the mercy of our Lord Jesus Christ to bring to you eternal life."

1 Corinthians 12:8 says it is the Holy Spirit who supplies our Christian gifts, "for to one is given the word of wisdom through the Spirit, to another the word of knowledge through the same Spirit, to another faith by the same Spirit, to other gifts of healings by the same Spirit, to another the working of miracles, to another prophecy, to another discerning of spirits, to another different kind of tongues, to another the interpretation of tongues. But one and the same Spirit works all these things, distributing to each one individually as He wills." If you like to be successful then you must be a friend of God as will guarantee your protection against the devil, as the devil does not like your success at all.

Chapter 3

Name and Blood of our Lord Jesus Christ

Name of Jesus Christ as a Weapon

First things first; Let us unpack what Jesus Christ means. Jesus means messiah, the one who takes away your sins and my sins. ***John 6:58*** says, *"This is the bread which came down from heaven—not as your fathers ate the manna and are dead. He who eats this bread will live forever."* Although he is a spirit, he was given the body purposely to take away our sins in the flesh as no human being was holy and willing to die for us and there were no animals' sacrifices that were able to please God to remove our sins in the flesh. ***Matthew 1:21*** says, "She will give birth to a son, and you are to give him the name Jesus because he will save his people from their sins." The bible tells us that by his stripes we were healed. While we were all sinners Christ died for us for God not to remember our sins in the flesh.

Christ means Spirit that gives life. ***John 6:63:*** *"It is the Spirit who gives life; the flesh profits nothing. The words that I speak to you are spirit, and they are*

life." So, Christ means the spirit that gives life to humankind. We know a human is a spirit in a body and with a soul. Christ laid down his own life to give us (humankind) our own lives through his own life. John 1:4: "In Him was life, and the life was the light of men." It is his death on the cross that enables the spirit (Holy Spirit) to be released by God for us (humanity). We are qualified to as children of God through the baptism of the Holy Spirit. Our lives have been saved by Christ to have peace with God.

The people of the world who had once lived in the darkness have seen a great light, because of the birth of our Lord Jesus Christ. He was born to distinguish light from the darkness. He was born to distinguish good from the bad. He was born to give hope, peace, love, and unity to millions of Christians across the world. He was born to set free all the lame, blind, deaf, mute and all other forms of oppression that Satan had put humanity through. Whatever you are going through today whether a family crisis, financial difficulties, sickness, loneliness, war, natural disaster, or any other forms of Satanic oppression. I have come to tell you that Jesus Christ has already set you free from the above-mentioned curses of rebellion against God. We live and continue to be sustained by his life on earth. Without him, we can do nothing. All you must do is to claim your freedom by faith.

The name of Jesus Christ is the only name under heaven by which a person can be saved. But not only that, it is also the name Satan fear if you apply it in your situation. Furthermore, it is through his name, flesh, and blood that you have peace with God. This is very critical for your walk with God, as he will not accept any other name, religion, or faith, by which you can be saved. People who get offended by this will end up losing their salvation from God. Not only is Jesus Christ the only son of God alone but all of us who have accepted Jesus Christ as our personal saviour becomes sons and daughters of God as well. Having said that, I know why it is so powerful in our minds because I once asked the same question, about how Jesus Christ can be a son of God when he was a human being born of flesh and blood? But that question had to fade away with time through the helped of the Holy Spirit who taught me many scriptures about Jesus Christ, particularly the book of the gospel of John. But I want you to ask yourself this now; if God created us in his own image, then why is it hard for him to create for himself a son in his own image? For God to deal with our sins in flesh, he had to send his son in the flesh to come and deal with the issue of our sins in the flesh which the animal sacrifices were not able to take way. The flesh and blood of Jesus Christ was the only thing that defeated the devil. He was obedient to death without rebelling and or sinning against God, the case no human being was capable of without being defeated by Satan.

Sin came into the world through Adam, and sin was taken out of the world through Jesus Christ. The authority of the world was handed over to Satan by Adam in the Garden of Eden. Sorrowfully before Jesus came, humankind was drowned in the sin of Adam and found itself irreconcilable to God. God had terminated the relationship between himself and humankind in the Garden of Eden through the rebellion of Adam and Eve. Humans became enemies of God. It is to be noticed that humans wilfully chose to work with Satan over God. This annoyed God greatly that humans chose to worship the creature than the creator. For the relationship to be restored, it required blood. This, for example, was seen in the old testament where animal sacrifices were required to cleanse the Israelites of their sins. To that effect, no priest could approach the holy of holies without blood in his hands or he would die. For life is in the blood, and for sinful people to be forgiven by God, it required the blood of animals. This did not please God as people continued to sin thereafter. Indeed, the blood of animals slaughtered each year for people's sins became irrelevant and ineffective as cleansing agents for sins. And for this reason, God had to send his son in the form of a human being to live among us and die for us. With this God was pleased. Unlike the animals' blood offered as an atonement for sins each year, Jesus Christ's blood became the atonement for our sins once and for all. It is through the blood of the son of God that we as humankind became presentable to God once again as holy and blameless. So, when you come before God as a Christian, know that your sins have been forgiven whether small or big. God has done it for you. The bible is unequivocally clear on this:

"Nor is there salvation in any other, for there is no other name under heaven given among men by which we must be saved" (Acts 4:12).

"For there is one God and one Mediator between God and men, the Man Christ Jesus, who gave Himself a ransom for all ..." (1 Timothy 2:5).

"There is one body and one Spirit ... one Lord, one faith, one baptism, one God and Father of all, who is above all, and through all, and in you all" (Ephesians 4:4).
Jesus said to him, "I am the way, the truth, and the life. No one comes to the Father except through Me" (John 14:6).

"I am the door. If anyone enters by Me, he will be saved, and will go in and find pasture ... I have come that they may have life and that they may have it more abundantly." (John 10:9-10).

Jesus said to her, "I am the resurrection and the life, he who believes in Me, though he may die, he shall live. And whoever lives and believes in Me shall never die" (John 11:25).

Then Jesus spoke to them again, saying, "I am the light of the world. He who follows Me shall not walk in darkness, but have the light of life" (John 8:12).

And Jesus said to them, "I am the bread of life. He who comes to Me shall never hunger and he who believes in Me shall never thirst" (John 6:35).

"I am the living bread which came down from heaven. If anyone eats of this bread, he will live forever; and the bread that I shall give is My flesh, which I shall give for the life of the world" (John 6:51).

"Whoever believes in Him should not perish but have eternal life. For God so loved the world that He gave His only begotten Son, that whoever believes in Him should not perish but have everlasting life" (John 3:15-16).

"He who believes in the Son has everlasting life; and he who does not believe the Son shall not see life, but the wrath of God abides on him" (John 3:36).

"Therefore I said to you that you will die in your sins; for if you do not believe that I am He, you will die in your sins" (John 8:24).

"Most assuredly, I say to you, he who hears My word and believes in Him who sent Me has everlasting life, and shall not come into judgment, but has passed from death to life" (John 5:24).

"And this is the testimony: that God has given us eternal life and this life is in His Son. He who has the Son has life; He who does not have the Son of God does not have life" (1 John 5:11).

"And we have seen and testify that the Father has sent the Son as Saviour of the world. Whoever confesses that Jesus is the Son of God, God abides in him, and he in God" (1 John 4:14).

The reason why I overloaded you with these scriptures is that Jesus Christ is the only way to God if you are to have your salvation. Without Christ, there is no salvation and more importantly no life in you. The only way you can go to battle against Satan and win is to accept this important fact. Read this very carefully: Jesus Christ is the only way to God. He had offered Himself as the only acceptable sacrifice to God on behalf of humanity-what a love. There is no salvation outside the name of Jesus Christ by which humankind will be saved. Controversial as it may be, but that is the reality many religions of the world such as Islam and Judaism and many more, must sit with or grapple with. This assertion was not made by any man but Jesus Christ himself when was here on earth. It is a fact many Christians should not shy away from but declare with boldness to the non-Christians, that they may be saved before it is too late. **For there is one God and one mediator between God and humanity, the man Christ Jesus (1 Timothy 2:5).** His mission here on earth was to save humans who were enslaved by the devil. He was here to preach the message of the kingdom of God to the blind, deaf, lame, and lowly in society. There was no pleasure at all for Jesus Christ to be crucified on the cross without resistance, as he was powerful and with powerful angels who could have wiped off the world in a minute. He had legions of angels, but he submitted to the cross without a fight. Think about that. Not only Jesus Christ but all of us as human beings are of God because God is present in us in the form of Spirit and soul. I wish people would get this message for their soul to be saved.

You are a new creation in Christ. *(2 Corinthians 5:17).* Knowing your identity in Christ not only gives you the power to live a victorious Christian life but to also defeat the devil in whatever accusations he brings against you in this life. Those Christians that live miserable lives are the ones that have not understood their identity in Christ. If you do not know who you are in Christ, the devil will get the opportunity to create guilt and caused you to question your salvation through Christ. If you are a born-again child of God, I want you to know that you are no longer in flesh but in Christ who lives in you. As you become a Christian, your spirit and soul comes into being reunited with God in Christ and you become spiritually alive again in God. When you are in Christ you must leave behind all those fleshly things such as drug addictions, envy, jealousy, drunkenness, gossip, slander, offence, adultery, fornication and so much more with which the devil tries to entice you again. The bible says that it is very hard for those who have accepted Jesus Christ as their personal saviour to sin because the spirit of God lives in them. The job of the Holy Spirit among other things is to keep you away from or to stir you out of sin if you have already sinned. If indeed the spirit of God dwells in you, you become a child of light, because in him there is no darkness. More importantly, as he executes it, you have the responsibility to cooperate with him in setting you free from the sin you have just committed, or the future sins you are going to commit. He will give you a warning before you commit sin, and it is your responsibility to discern his voice. If you love God, and you do not want to offend him again then you must stay away from sin in order for the spirit of God to dwell in you forever. Your attitudes, responses, reactions, and actions are greatly affected by what you believe Christ did for you on the cross to be set free from the bondage of death by Satan.

"Truth," is a spiritual being. *(John 14:6).* Unless this spiritual being is in you, you will struggle to know the truth, understanding the truth, speaking the truth, and maintaining the truth within you. Jesus Christ is the truth. The world today continues to struggle to know what really the truth is. How to say the truth and maintain the truth. If I may ask you today, what is the truth according to you? And I imagine your answers to be along this line: truth is what I believe to be real to me; the truth is what others in agreement with me say and believe to be true; the truth is the facts-based principles supported by evidence over a matter, situation, or thing. These definitions as to what the truth is plus other answers you could give me, do make sense and have elements of reality in them as to what really is the truth. Yes, these definitions are partly correct, but they are not the true definition of what truth is.

Interestingly as well, these definitions of truth are also undermined or devalued by these sayings; what is true to you may not be true to me, and there is no such thing as a right or wrong answer (meaning there is no true one collective definition of truth.) Sometimes people who would want to know what really is the truth begin to ponder and ask a question; What then is the truth if it can be watered down like this? I want you to know today that you are not alone. I was once in this state of confusion to define the truth. But today I have good news for you as to what is the true definition of truth.

Note: Here is the true definition of truth. Truth is a "spiritual being" who stays in you and enables you to believe, speak and maintain the truth. Truth is a person. Truth is Jesus Christ. Jesus Christ said in the book of John 14:6, "I am the truth". When Jesus Christ is in you, the truth is in you. Truth is a strong weapon of your defence against the lies or deception directed at you by Satan. Truth becomes your standing ground against all lies when you know and believe that there is the Holy Spirit, Jesus Christ, and God almighty. Truth also becomes your standing ground when you believe what the bible says about the origin of all things (both living and nonliving). With this in mind, you can liberate yourself from all the lies in the world today. If you are Christian, you must admit the fact that Jesus Christ is the truth, and you will not be deceived or struggle to tell the truth and stand up for the truth. When you receive new information contradicting this fact then you must always dismiss it by referring to the bible as the source of your truth. Jesus Christ said in the book of ***John 17:17***, "Sanctify them by your truth. Your word (the bible) is the truth". If the opportunity presents itself to you to compromise this fact, then you must avoid it. You must have this rule of thumb: if it is true, join it and defend it, but if it is a lie then get out of it. Truth must be the first line of your defence against the devil.

The alternative to the truth lies in another spiritual being. I also want you to know that there is another spiritual being called a liar. When this spiritual being is in you, who is Satan, he enables you to speak the lies, defend the lies and struggle to tell the truth because there is no truth in him according to Jesus Christ. Satan is the biggest liar of all times. He has been lying and he has lied from the beginning of creation according to the bible. As he did to Adam and Eve, in the Garden of Eden, he will also do the same to you today by giving you twisted information: half-truth and half-lie. Because he knows if he had to give you a complete lie you would discover it straight away and avoid it. For example, he will not tell you to go and kill a person, so he builds anger within you that turns into a rage that enables you to kill the person. The bible says ***when the devil speaks lies he speaks from his nature because he is the father of all lies (John 8:44).*** Lying is the main problem today in the world as people try to defend themselves from their mistakes through lies. I want you to know from today that lying is what Satan will use to keep you in bondage. Keep away from lies and you will be free.

"And you shall know the truth, and the truth shall make you free." (***John 8:32).*** Jesus Christ is the truth. Let him live in you and you will never struggle to say the truth.

"Jesus Christ has set you free from the bondage of sin." Never let sin again rule in your mortal body. Whatever you are going through – sickness, depression, stress, anxiety, aloneness, discouragement, or disappointment, let it not rule over you as it has no right over you. Everyday decree and declare the blood and name of Jesus Christ over your situation and it will be gone forever.

The Blood of Jesus Christ as a Weapon

The blood of Jesus is the blood of the covenant between God and mankind. The salvation of souls would not have been accomplished without the blood of Jesus Christ. The only remission of our sins against God is through the blood of our Lord Jesus Christ. All the requirements of our sins have been removed by the blood and name of Jesus Christ. All you need to do is to decree and declare the blood and name of Jesus Christ over your situation and will see the move of God in your life. **Revelations 12:11 says, "And they overcame him [Satan] by the blood of the Lamb and by the word of their testimony, and they did not love their lives to the death."**

I would like to open for you three things in this verse that enable us to overcome the devil, which are the blood of Jesus, the testimony of Jesus and the love of Jesus. The lamb in this verse refers to Jesus Christ, who was killed before the foundation of the earth. *(Revelations 5:12).* This verse is proof that God had to plan things ahead of time knowing that Adam and Eve will be deceived by Satan upon creating and putting them in the garden of Eden, and so he will correct that by sending him to die for them to redeem their offspring from death. Before we go into the discussion about the blood in detail, I want to draw your attention to the former practice in Israel, where the atonement of sin was through the animal sacrifices. In that tradition animal sacrifice was the solution for humanity's sins against God. Once an animal was killed, the sins of that man were removed by God. This was the practice before the messiah came to die for them (Jews) and us (Gentiles).

Why blood for sin? Because the blood is the life of all living things. So, giving the blood of animals on the behalf of man a person's sins was exchanging the life of that person with the life of the animal. Hence, the animal had to die instead of the person because of the person's sins. Unlike the blood of animals, which did not remove the sins of the person permanently from them, the blood of Jesus Christ did. Why the blood of Jesus? Because his blood was free of sin. I hope now you understand the concept of blood and where it came from.

To this effect, God had to correct the reoccurring issue of sins in the blood and flesh of humanity by sending his son to the earth in the likeness of humanity (with blood and flesh), to correct the issue of sins in the blood and flesh. Jesus Christ being a hundred per cent man had to die on our behalf and exchange his life for our lives as we were dead in sins. The stronghold of the devil against humankind was the issue of sin in the flesh and blood of humankind. The devil knows very well that God hates sins and obviously he will not tolerate humankind with sin in their flesh and blood for a cordial relationship to occur between them and him. Once you get this then the devil will lose his grip on you. When Jesus Christ died on the cross he dealt with your sins and mine, restoring us back to God. So, peace was made between God and us through Jesus Christ. When you remind the devil about the blood of Jesus Christ as an atonement of your sins, he will flee from you knowing that God will not accept his accusations of your sins against you in heaven. When you come before God in prayer admitting your sins before him, God knows that he has already dealt with the issue of your sins through his own son Jesus Christ, and so the devil is out of the equation here (disarmed and powerless against you). The power of the devil is to bring accusations against you before God regarding your sins, but when you admit them before God, then Satan is a loser. I hope you understand this, so your life will be changed forever.

The second way you can overcome the devil in this verse is through the testimony "**the word of your testimony.**" (*Revelations 12:11).* Testimony means going through a test to testify about it. We must go first through a test in order for us to, later on, talk about it. Whatever you go through in life is an opportunity for you to testify. Whatever, God has rescued you out of or from is your opportunity to talk about that goodness of God. Many people once they get themselves into problems with the devil, in which it becomes very difficult for them to deal with, cry out loud to God, for help, but once that is done by God in their favour, they quickly forget what God has done for them or for that matter never talks about it to others. The reason why our testimony is a weapon against the devil is that it will help bring hope to others who are going through the same situation as you. But not only that, but we can also secure God's future protections against us from the devil. You must proclaim, speak, confess, and declare what God has done for you in the church of God, at your workplace, and your other social function outlets. This is not only for God glory but for his rewards back to you. Even in the social setting, who does not want to be acknowledged for what he has done to his fellow human beings? You need to talk to others about your relationship, job, wrong decisions, food, starvation, wars, accidents, that God has rescued you out of. If it would not have been for God, you would not have survived the demonic attacks in these areas of your life, which would have paralysed you forever. Ultimately you must not forget to talk about Jesus Christ to relatives, friends, and colleagues because this is all through him. The reason why God set us free from our conditions is to be future sources of hope to those who may be going through the same situation just as yours in future or the generations following you and beyond. Your history of victory over your deadly situation can have an impact on other people lives.

The third way you can overcome the devil in this verse is through love "**they did not love their lives to the death.**" *(Revelations 12:11).* Love is the bond perfection of all things. Love does not seek to harm its neighbour or his properties. When you love people, it is very hard for the devil to get you and defeat you. Through love, you can always overcome bad with the good. If your intentions against your fellow human beings are always pure you will never stumble in your walk with God. When you know what Christ has done for you for free, then you will always do things in gratitude to your fellow humans and to God. In other words, it is very hard to offend God if you have the love of God in you. When you treat God as your Daddy, and you do what he says, then you know that he will be happy with you, then you can easily defeat the devil. When you operate in this truth then nothing can overcome you. All sins that we commit lead to death, and if we love our lives then we must keep away from sins. There are some temptations that we can avoid by keeping away from sin. The devil knows that if he can get you to sin, then he will get you out of God's protection zone. The only way the devil can kill you is when you have lost God's protection around you through sin. This is not saying that we are pure, and we cannot sin, but when we do sin, then we must admit that we have sinned before God, as the devil will come and accuse us before God.

Can I ask you this question: What is the point of hiding your sins from God, when you know that he already knows them when you have committed them?

These three weapons are powerful when you proclaim them against Satan: the blood, your love or relationship with the Lord, and your word of testimony. As a matter of fact, when Satan knows you know these weapons, he has nothing else with which to defeat you. He is a defeated liar, and you should think and act like it. I like this statement from the great man of God, Dr Tony Evans, "The blood of Jesus Christ is a passport that gives believers legal access and authority in the spiritual realm".

Chapter 4

Prayer

God cannot do anything for you unless you pray. God will never intervene in your situation until you pray. If you want God to protect you continually you must pray continually without ceasing. Prayer is the only channel through which you can access all your provisions from God. If you want your sickness to be healed, pray. If you want your family relationship to be restored, pray. Pray- pray- pray to God. I cannot emphasise this enough; God cannot intervene in the affairs of people until they pray. ***Jeremiah 29:11-14 – "For I know the thoughts that I think toward you, says the Lord, thoughts of peace and not of evil, to give you a future and a hope. Then you will call upon Me and go and pray to Me, and I will listen to you. And you will seek me and find me when you search for Me with all your heart. I will be found by you, says the Lord, and I will bring you back from your captivity; I will gather you from all the nations and from all the places where I have driven you, says the Lord, and I will bring you to the place from which I cause you to be carried away captive."***

Although God almighty is ready to answer our prayers there are guidelines and procedures, principles, rules, and regulations we must first meet for God to answer every single prayer we pray for in him. We must take prayer as a serious business when we want to be prayer warriors that are responded to by God. In everything we do, we must master its tactics, secrets, ways, and specifics that govern it – in this case, prayer also has ways and tactics you need in order to be answered by God. These specifics of prayer are listed below:

You must have Personal Relationship with God
We must establish a good, intimate personal relationship with God if we want him to answer our prayers every time we pray. The reason why God created humankind in the first place was to have an intimate relationship with him. Above all else he wants us to approach him and establish a one-on-one personal relationship with him. He has incredible love that needs to continue if we are to achieve much in this life on earth. We must consult him every time we have a problem to solve in our lives because he will have better solutions for our problems than we think and perform. The same longing, we have among ourselves as human beings and particularly among the members of the opposite sex is the same relationship God is longing for between us and him. For example, people want to have good, spouses, children, friends, colleagues, bosses, leaders, and businesspeople that can understand us and ones that we can relate with. This longing was proven to us by God almighty when he had to send his only begotten son to come and die for us to restore his relationship with us. That is how serious God is about our relationship with him.

The intensity of this relationship according to God is that it must be a 24/7 conversation that is over many issues we want to discuss with him, no matter whether they are big or small. On many occasions, Christians fail to establish this ongoing relationship with God and when disaster hits, we just want to rush to him expecting quick answers to our problems and thereafter stop this relationship. According to my own observation, most Christians think that this relationship is just established when they go to church on Sundays, sing a few songs in church, pay tithes, read the Bible occasionally, pray and fast, and that that will be enough for God to be their friend. No, this is not how God wants it. He wants to talk to us seven days a week. It is only God that can give you perfect, pure, true, and unconditional love that you badly chase from other human beings. People will always fail you, but God will never fail you.

The Will of God

Before we come to God, he already knew us and had already predestined us with a perfect plan for our lives on earth. Unless our prayer lines up with this perfect will of God for us he will not answer our prayer. Because it is not about what you want to do on earth for yourself but what he wants you to do on earth for him. God knows what is best for every situation you find yourself in - you do not. God knows what your future holds for you - you do not. And finally, God's wisdom and knowledge are always better than ours in every situation we find ourselves in. If any of our prayers are not answered by God, it is because what we ask God is not what God wants us to have. This is the perfect verse in the bible that tells us this condition.

"Now this is the confidence that we have in him, that if we ask anything according to his will, he hears us. And if we know that he hears us, whatever we ask, we know that we have the petitions that we have asked of him" (1 John 5:14).

Additionally, you do not know what to pray for or how to pray for it, so the best way to pray according to the will of God is through the Holy Spirit. This is the definite assurance that your prayer will be in the will of God and be answered according to the will of God because the Holy Spirit knows your mind well and he knows the will of God that you need in your life. But you must first establish your relationship with him so that you can be sensitive to his voice and his instructions on how you need to pray. So, make the Spirit of God your friend and you will save a lot of your time and your energy in your prayer life.

There are also situations in which you know what you want for your life, which is perfect already in the will of God, then you can go ahead and pray to God about it. For example, you have already established a business that has just collapsed, and you want God to restore it, you can go ahead and pray to God about the restoration of your failed business. This way you are sure that this is the perfect will of God that you will have resources to sustain yourself and your family and to a larger extent others, by sowing into them through almsgiving, tithes, offerings, and seeds.

God Will Hear the Prayers of the Righteous

Listen to me: the only way God almighty will hear our prayer is if we are righteous before him. We must keep away from doing the wrong things and do the right things always. Although we are standing on the righteousness of Christ, we must first turn away from doing evil or wrong things to qualify for the righteousness of Christ. By either avoiding or repenting from our sins we can obtain Christ righteousness. We must do what is pleasing to God in him for him to hear and answer our prayers. The only way he will hear us is when we are keeping his commandments, judgments, statutes, laws that govern our human conduct. Here are four major verses of the bible pointing to this fact:

"The Lord is far from the wicked, but He hears the prayer of the righteous" (Proverbs 15:29).

"And whatever we ask we receive from Him because we keep His commandments and do those things that are pleasing in His sight" (1 John 3:22).

"The effective, fervent prayer of a righteous man or woman avails much" (James 5:16).

"Let him turn away from evil and do good; let him seek peace and pursue it. For the eyes of the Lord are on the righteous, and His ears are open to their prayers, but the face of the Lord is against those who do evil" (1 Peter 3:11).

It is imperative to know that it will not be healthy and productive for you to continue to deal with sins when you have found the Lord Jesus Christ. The reason he died for us is that we may live our lives free of sins because he hates sins. The fact he die**d** for us shows that he wants us to live our lives free of sins in order to receive his full redemption. God does not entertain sins for a minute, and if you want to continue to remain in sins then you better know that you will never receive answers to prayers from him. Many people at times try to hide their sins from God thinking that God does not know their private life, yet they forget that he is the one who created them and has the law of conscience governing their hearts from right and wrong. The only way you can receive your blessings from God is through the state of your heart it does not matter whether you are a Christian or not a Christian. Let alone God answering our prayers, the bible says that he will hide his face from us if we continue to commit sin. For example, you cannot claim to be in a righteous state with God when you are secretly cheating on your spouse, verbally or physically abusing your children, taking drugs, binge drinking, gossiping about others with your friends and so many other possible sins you are committing. If you continue in any of these or others, then know that God cannot be mocked, and the only person you are cheating is yourself. The bible is clear on this; the only way God can answer your prayers is if you come to him in the sincerity of heart knowing that he knows what is in secret, and the only way he can listen to you is when you have confessed your sins before him.

Having unforgiving heart against other people is a recipe for an unanswered prayer. When you do not forgive then do not waste your time for a minute to pray to God as he will not answer your prayer. The bible says do not even approach the throne of God when you know there is a person in your life you are holding grudges against.

"And whenever you stand praying, if you have anything against anyone, forgive him, that your Father in heaven may also forgive you your trespasses. But if you do not forgive, neither will your Father in heaven forgive your trespasses" **(Mark 11:25).**

For those that have struggled to hear God's voice yet have prayed many times in their lives please consult the Holy Spirit to show you or to reveal to you whether there is a person or persons you are holding grudges against, that you might have forgotten. Unforgiveness is one of the major areas used by the devil to block your blessings from God because he knows God hates sins. It is true from many testimonies of great people of God that the Holy Spirit does show people their areas of unforgiven sin against other people if they consult with him. If you do not forgive then you will be stuck from moving to the next level in your journey with God. Note that your prayer is your daily communication with the Lord and if that does not work then that means you will achieve nothing much in your life.

The other thing that determines your prayer life with God is your family relationships. If the relationships between husband, wife, and their children, is bad, it can hinder your prayers from being answered by God. The bible teaches us that husbands must love their wives and give them due respect as weaker vessels, and wives must submit to their husbands (listening and doing what is right by their husbands), whereas children must listen to and respect their parents in order for them to have long lives on earth. This is the God-family glued together by the love of each other for them to be blessed by God. God treats the husband as the head of the family and if the wife and the children do not respect the father, then God will shut down their prayer line. That is why the family must be in order in our relationship with God. God wants a disciplined and respectful family that will never bring shame to his name. God wants himself glorified in our conduct with him just as we ourselves want to glorify him if our children and the rest of our family members respect God's ways and conduct themselves according to his desires for them.

Stating Your Case Before God

This statement may look very controversial, yet a reality that people who want God in their lives must face. The reason God wants us to present our case to him is not that he does not know it, but rather he wants you to acknowledge that he exists, and you can enter a personal relationship with him for life. To put this in context, you cannot call a person from your mobile number that you are not sure will answer you. The only person you have the desire and interest to call is the person you are sure will answer your call no matter what may be-on his part. The reason God wants us to state our case before him is because he wants to be our best lifetime friend before our other earthly friends. Once you have established this relationship with God then you must state your desired prayer requests to him over the specific need you want him to answer. There are always reasons and desires for your hearts for the things you want to achieve in this life, or that you want God to partner with for them to come to fruition. Without God's partnership with you, it will be difficult if not possible for you to achieve them alone as the devil will not allow them for you. So, state your unique case as to why you need God's help with your job, money, family, business, love, joy, happiness, power, strength, health and so on. For example, when going for a job interview, you are always prepared to answer questions that you may be asked by the interviewer in order for you to prove yourself that you are competent and have all it takes to do the job. You must prove yourself to the interviewer that you need the job, and you are qualified for it. The same applies to God; he wants you to state your case for that specific prayer request for your need.

The bible teaches us that God is not a respecter of man or woman and he will never show partiality or favouritism to anyone who has not asked him and stated his or her case in prayer. As a matter of fact, prayer is the only way we can access our needs from him, and every single person must pray no matter who they are. One thing on which one must rest assured is that God will answer the prayer of righteousness offered to him in good faith, by stating reasons for the desired results. In fact, God invites you to reason with him on the matters you are going through. He wants you to have a dialogue with him over the best outcome for you. All the promises of God are yes and amen in him for his glory. *(1 Corinthians 1:20).* And for this reason, he will never fail to grant to you the best desires of your heart so long as they are in your best interest and according to his perspective. God almighty will even sometimes forgive other sinful people for his trustworthy servant if they present a strong case to him over a certain matter. In brief, you must put together your case and reasons and contend for it in order for God to grant it to you. You may ask, is this possible? Well, if it was possible for Moses then why not you? Unless you are not a committed fervent servant of God. Remember God was angry with the Israelites when they moulded the golden calf as their God, while Moses went to the Lord at Mount Sinai to receive the ten commandments. God wanted to destroy them, but Moses petitioned God to forgive and spare their lives from destruction. And as a result, God granted Moses the desire of his heart according to the strong case he stated before God that Egyptians and their leader pharaoh would say that God did took the Israelites out of Egypt to go and kill them.

Exodus 32:11-14- "Then Moses pleaded with the Lord his God, and said: "Lord, why does Your wrath burn hot against Your people whom You have brought out of the land of Egypt with great power and with a mighty hand? "Why should the Egyptians speak, and say, 'He brought them out to harm them, to kill them in the mountains, and to consume them from the face of the earth'? "Remember Abraham, Isaac, and Israel, Your servants, to whom You swore by Your own self, and said to them, 'I will multiply your descendants as the stars of heaven; and all this land that I have spoken of I give to your descendants, and they shall inherit it forever.' " So the Lord relented from the harm which He said He would do to His people."

Ask – Seek – Knock

The reason why I personally believe many people miss out or prematurely quit their walk with the Lord is because of the above mentioned three processes: that people treated them as one process or had no idea about them altogether. If you are a committed Christian, then I want you to know that these are three distinct processes and stages that God wants us to go through in our desire to walk with him. Let me make this observation now: it is very hard to find God if you are not hungry for him. And one of the ways of seeking him is through unrelenting prayer in the sequences of asking, seeking, and knocking. Unless these processes are complete, you can never claim to have known God. I believe that these three principles have shown the way to us on how we can approach God almighty in our own prayer life with him, on every single issue on every single occasion.

Every time you ask God with a sincere heart on an issue, he will let you know whether you can go through the three processes or any one of them each time. For those who have developed an inner connection with the Holy Spirit, you can ask him whether you need to go through all of them or any one of them. At times God, through the Holy Spirit, would want you to go into seeking and knocking mode if he does want to teach you deep things of God before he can grant you your prayer request. But we can be sure of one thing, that the spirit of God will guide us and direct us if we are to go into the seeking and knocking modes. For example, in real-life situations, you do not give up on one application for a job rejected by one company. Let us face it even if that company rejected you many times, you would love to still go back to them and find out why you were rejected. This will give you a tip on how to approach the next job application. This is why God will allow us to pray many times for us to learn new ways and new things in our prayer life with him.

I will discuss in detail these processes so that in future you cannot treat them as one process in your prayer life. I will show you from here that these processes are not one but totally different, which you must meet if your prayer request is not answered on the first occasion you prayed it.

"Ask, and it will be given to you; seek, and you will find; knock, and it will be opened to you. For everyone who asks receives, and he who seeks finds, and to him who knocks it will be opened … If you then, being evil, know how to give good gifts to your children, how much more will your Father who is in heaven give good things to those who ask Him!" (Matthew 7:7-11).

Asking

God cannot give us what we need until we ask him through prayer. This should not be a surprise to us because even in the ideal family setting, parents love those children who ask them things rather than those that take things illegally. The same applies to God; if you want something from him, then ask him once or twice. If what you are asking God is in His perfect will for you, then he will grant it to you on one occasion or twice when you pray to him. Because at times when we ask God for something, he may not grant **it** to us if it is not in his perfect will for us. We need to know that God is not like the Devil; he will not give us things that will destroy us. If we ask him for the wrong things, then he will not give them to us. For example, if you ask him to give you the job, and he knows what is in your heart is to later use the money to gamble then he will never give you the job. Besides, the reason why God will not grant us our desires until we have full surrender to him is that we can go and later boast and claim credit for it instead of praising God. The worst scenario is that we may even abandon our walk with him if we feel accomplished, forgetting then there is nothing we can pay him for our souls to be saved. No matter what you have you cannot pay for your own salvation to go and live with God in heaven. Here is the verse inviting us to ask God if we are in need and according to his will, not our will.

"Yet you do not have because you do not ask. You ask and do not receive, because you ask amiss, that you may spend it on your pleasures" (James 4:2).

Seeking

At times we may ask, and God may not respond to us, he may tell us to wait or he may say "no" altogether to what we are asking him in prayer. If this happens then he may want, you to go a little bit further into seeking or searching mode for more answers from him. The bible tells us that we must ask, seek, and find. So, you may be tempted not to seek in order to find. By going further in seeking, you will have a complete and better understanding of why God is silent on your request through prayer. You may ask, but where can I seek? There are many ways and means you can seek further answers from God if your prayer is not answered in the first instant you prayed it. For example, you can go into the further seeking of God through reading the bible, fasting, inquiring from the Holy Spirit if you have close intimacy with him, and you are able to listen to his voice and discern it. You can also listen to other people's testimonies with your similar case, listening to preachers and particularly great men of God who are being used by the Holy Spirit, and reading books written by great men of God in your subject matter.

The reason why many people miss out on the better blessings from God is that they are not willing to go into seeking mode let alone the knocking mode. The reason why God wants us to go through ask-seek-knock is in order to appreciate what he is giving us. It is a common occurrence that if we can find things easily in life then we do not appreciate them. We will always be tempted to boast about them glorifying in our own efforts instead of God's grace over our lives. So, we can claim credit and not God's grace. It may also be that he wants you to learn new things and new ways that will shape your thinking, speaking and conduct in life. It is through the seeking process that you may be humbled, and later attribute all your successes in this life to him. Make no mistake; what God will later give you after the seeking process will be the best for your life.

Knocking

Knocking mode in your prayer life is the last high-intensity level with God. In this step, you now have full confidence that God exists, and he can be in an intimate relationship with you. You are now so close to God and God is so close to you. You are now true friends in both physicality and spirituality. In physicality, if you have an issue that you need God for then you can rush to him and knock at his door in prayer. In spirituality, if God wants something to be done by you then he comes to you and tells you what to do and how to do it. You are now friends for life – this life and the life to come. In the natural setting, for example, you will be tempted not to open your door to the person knocking on it from outside. First, he would have spent a great deal of his time locating your place and second, he will have information for you. The same thing applies to God; he will open his door for you because while you were asking and seeking, he was there watching you to come into his presence. He knows now that you are serious, obedient, and willing to work with him. When you have arrived at this last step there is an absolute guarantee that God will open his door to you. But it is still his discretion whether to allow you in or to turn you away if he deems that you are not willing and obedient to work with him.

The Prayer of Agreement

Another powerful prayer demand is the prayer of agreement. This happens sometimes if the Lord wants us to embark on the big assignment that needs powerful prayers warriors and prayer dominations. For example, prayers such as for nations, natural disasters, and churches need collective efforts by many Christian prayer warriors. When you want to become a powerful prayer warrior, then you must hook up with other powerful great men and women of God, over huge prayer assignments from God. Can you imagine what would happen if two or three powerful great men/women of God converged at one place for one purpose and one cause? With these combined efforts they can enable breakthroughs of miracles from heaven. If Christians unite in harmony and in agreement over a specific task or assignment they ask from God, it will be granted to them. But only because Jesus Christ promised to be among them. If Jesus Christ is among you then what you ask in his presence will be granted straight away to you as he is the Lord of all answers.

Not only do you need prayer warriors for major assignments you will also need them in your own prayer life as they are much and more anointed than you by God, in their long-time service to the Lord. In this context, experience matters. God has raised these people for prayer as he raised prophets for inspirations. If you are a born-again Christian and new in your relationship with God, then you must find these prayerful men and women of God in order to have major breakthroughs in your prayers. This is not to say at all that one-on-one prayer life is not effective and powerful, but you can call people in if you are stranded or confused because your prayers are taking a long time to be answered by God. On many occasions God wants us to have one-on-one, close, intimate, and personal relationships with him in our prayer life. Like everyone else, you will be tempted not to have direct communication with your father of creation in order to have your own experiences and encounters with him.

"Again I say to you that if two of you agree on earth concerning anything that they ask, it will be done for them by My Father in heaven. For where two or three are gathered together in My name, I am there in the midst of them" (Matthew 18:19).

The Power of Intercessory Prayer

This is another prayer that demands a man, or a woman of God to know and to also use it. This prayer secret works best when God is angry with the nations and people of the nations. If he wants to completely destroy them, he needs an intercessor or intercessors who can stand in the gap in order to thaw God's wrath over certain conditions or situations. When a good friend of God stands in the gap between him and the nation or the person God has an issue with, God will be ready to answer their prayers. A good example of this is when the Israelites made a golden calf to be worshipped while Moses was away on the mountain with God to receive the ten commandments. When God saw their actions, he was furious and wanted to destroy them on the spot, but Moses stood in the gap on the behalf of the Israelites in order for God not to destroy them. Moses stood in the gap and requested God to allow them to repent in order not to kill them for their sins. This intercessory prayer demand indicates that God is willing not to destroy people when there are intercessors who are willing to stand in the gap between people or nations who have committed sins against him.

If you are willing to let God use you in this situation, then know that you will help, touch, heal and deliver a lot of people from adverse situations in which God would have destroyed people or nations. There is always a reward for this from God if you are willing to give your time, yourself, and your energy in such situations. Not only is this important for your rewards but it is also good for you to save some of your close family members such as spouse, children, siblings, parents, colleagues, and friends.

Praying for Something More Than One Time

Apart from the Lord himself whom we pray to, no one knows exactly how many times we should pray over an issue for God to answer us. This is a grey area where many Christians do not have a consensus on how to approach it and are left to individual one-on-one relationships with the Lord. At times based on individuals' accounts, when they go to God in prayer, it may be once or twice before God answers them. Many Christians go into prevailing prayer with God when they get God to answer their prayer by asking him many times over the same matter. This shows their seriousness to God that they are not willing to relent until their prayer is answered over the same issue. This will get God to move quickly on your behalf if he is seeing you committed to him in prayers shedding tears, sweating, spending time and your energy over the matter in your prayer room. For instance, Jacob had to wrestle with God for the whole night until dawn over his blessings; although he was injured, he never gave up on God until he was finally blessed by God. So, you can see how hard it may be sometimes to get God's blessings over your life.

This does not even end here. There is in the bible what is called fervent prayer. This means it is not a one-off prayer but indicating elements of some intensity. An example is when the prophet Elijah prayed for rain in Israel, he knew it was not a one-off thing as he had to send his servant to check on the cloud seven times before the rain came.

Furthermore, St. Paul says that we must pray without ceasing in the book of 1 Thessalonians 5:16; "Rejoice always, **pray without ceasing**, in everything give thanks." This verse is telling us that we must pray without stopping until we have received our answers from God over the matter, we have requested from him. This verse may also mean that we must pray continuously in our walk with God even though our prayers are answered by him over the matter or not. Through your determination, persistence, and intense desire to have God answer your prayers, without doubt, you will have many of your prayers answered. In my own opinion, there is no harm in approaching God over an issue more than one time, so long as it is within his will for your life. It may also be good to consult the Holy Spirit over the matter on how to approach God if you have an intimate relationship with him as it will save your time in your prayer room. Overall, what is important in this matter is to pray to God if you want something from him. It is only through prayer that God not only answers us but also communicates with us.

"The effective, fervent prayer of a righteous man avails much. Elijah was a man with a nature like ours, and he prayed earnestly that it would not rain, and it did not rain on the land for three years and six months. And he prayed again, and the heaven gave rain, and the earth produced its fruit" (James 5:16-18).

Do Not Lose Heart

The greatest mistake you will make is to quit, thinking that God is silent over your request. No matter what, never quit on God. You see, the difference between God and the Devil is that God will never give you things prematurely, as the Devil does if they are to destroy you. He wants first to train you in his ways in order to have confidence in you and to relate with him before he releases your blessings. No matter what, his thoughts and ways regarding your situations will always be the best for you. Sometimes we think God is silent when he is actually speaking to us and we are not hearing him. The spirit of God is speaking to you; just pay attention to your innermost beings; your dreams, visions, word of knowledge and senior preachers of his words are the ways God is speaking to you while you are awaiting your blessings.

When a heavy storm is on us or any of our relatives, we must continue to pray earnestly without ceasing to God if we are to receive a breakthrough from him. We must go into this prayer without the intention to quit or to lose heart when things get difficult. Sometimes God may be watching you to see how serious you are in your prayer request from him. He is watching your heart to see whether you have doubt or seriousness about your prayer request to him. As a matter of fact, he is testing your patience, resilience, determination, and your efforts to continue to pray to him for a while before he responds to you.

In the parable of the unjust judge and the persistent widow, our Lord Jesus Christ has revealed to us an important secret of continuous prayers in four key ideas; you always ought to pray, do not lose heart, continually come, and cry out day and night to God the father in order for him to answer our prayers. According to this parable, the unjust judge was not ready and willing to resolve the case of the widow woman, but due to the persistence of the woman, the judge just gave in and resolved her case in order for her to stop bothering him and not to come to him every day. This is exactly what the Lord does sometimes if he sees in your heart that you are not serious or doubt whether he will answer your prayers. In our own personal prayer to God, we must always pray, and not lose heart and quit in the middle before God answers our prayers. We must cry to him day and night in order for him to have mercy for us. We must instead go into heavy mighty prevailing prayers with the Lord seeking more answers from him about our situation. This powerful prayer of persistence could be used in dire and severe situations such as; dying/unsaved relatives, drug addictions, false religious deceptions and terminal diseases like cancer, Ebola, and Aids. Below are the verses in the book of Luke 18, where these powerful prayer secrets are revealed to us by Lord Jesus Christ:

"Then He spoke a parable to them, that men always ought to pray and not lose heart, saying: "There was in a certain city a judge who did not fear God nor regard man. Now there was a widow in that city; and she came to him, saying, 'Avenge me of my adversary.'
And he would not for a while; but afterwards, he said within himself, 'Though I do not fear God nor regard man, yet because this widow troubles me I will avenge her, lest by her continual coming she weary me.'"

Then the Lord said, "Hear what the unjust judge said. And shall God not avenge His own elect who cry out day and night to Him, though He bears long with them? I tell you that He will avenge them speedily. Nevertheless, when the Son of Man comes, will He really find faith on the earth?" (Luke 18:1-8).

The Intercessory Ministries of Jesus Christ and the Holy Spirit

If you have not known this before then you will be one of the most blessed human beings to come across this book. One of the most revealing ways in our prayer life with God is that, if we are sincere in our hearts and showing seriousness with God in asking, seeking, and knocking at his door, the Holy Spirit and even our Lord Jesus Christ will help us in our prayers to God. Remember prayer is our communication with God and so they will help us communicate with God even very quickly. You are blessed if you seek God wholeheartedly and are hungry for his knowledge. To put this **in** context, when you pray, the Holy Spirit will help you channel your prayer into the will of God for your life, and Jesus Christ will be there with you, presenting your case before the father in heaven. What a revelation. You see why I told you early that you should never quit on God, but if you know how to approach him it will be a lot easier for you. But all of these are dependent upon your heart. As children of the highest God, we have the right to ask help from the Lord Jesus Christ and the Holy Spirit to help us at difficult moments in our lives where we are facing danger. At the difficult moments of our lives such as sickness and particularly when we do not have the energy and voice to pray, the Holy Spirit will pray for us and encourage us to stay in our hope with Christ our saviour.

If you find yourself in a very difficult situation where you do not even know how to pray and what to pray for, just ask the Holy Spirit to connect you to our Lord Jesus Christ in prayer. Just as you would do with other believers by joining in prayers for them or for you, the same thing will happen if you involve Jesus Christ and the Holy Spirit in your prayer request to the God almighty. But this will only happen if you are sincere in your heart and your prayer request is within the will of God. By having the Holy Spirit channel your prayer request in the will of God and having Jesus Christ present it before the father in heaven, your chances of having a breakthrough at every difficult situation are very high. The bible tells us that Jesus Christ can intercede for us to God the father. This means that Jesus Christ can pray on our behalf if there is a need to do so in complicated cases of our prayers. For example, we are not sure about our future, but both the Holy Spirit and our Lord Jesus Christ can intercede for us in advance in order to avoid future calamities from befalling us. This is the heaviest prayer demand I have ever known. This will be a great prayer secret for unexpected difficult situations such as that one of the nations who are away from the will of God-having wars, internal divisions, and internal civil strife.

If you find yourself being led by the Holy Spirit or if you want the Holy Spirit to lead you in your prayers the following will happen: what to pray for and how to pray will change; the verses to use in prayer and the wordings of your prayers will change; the time to pray and the strategy to pray will change; the approach to God and how many times to pray over the matter will change, and you will know whether there is something you need to do at your end before your prayer is answered and whether to call in another great person of God to join you in your prayers. All of these will be revealed by the Holy Spirit. This will lessen your prayer time with God if the Spirit of God is involved in your prayers. So, make friendship with him. In your walk with the Holy Spirit, you will be able to know beforehand whether certain prayer requests are worthy to be brought before the Lord or not. The spirit will lead you and teach you to become sensitive to his instructions and discernment of his voice when he speaks to you on what he wants you to do. Below are the verses in the bible in support of these arguments:

Who is he who condemns? It is Christ who died, and furthermore is also risen, who is even at the right hand of God, who also makes intercession for us" (Romans 8:34).

"Therefore, He is also able to save to the uttermost those who come to God through Him, since He ever lives to make intercession for them" (Hebrews 7:25).

"Likewise, the Spirit also helps in our weaknesses. For we do not know what we should pray for as we ought, but the Spirit Himself makes intercession for us with groanings which cannot be uttered. Now He who searches the hearts knows what the mind of the Spirit is because He makes intercession for the saints according to the will of God" (Romans 8:26-27).

Mighty Prevailing Prayer

This is a prayer you take to God with intensity and seriousness. With this prayer, you have one mindset: to have God answer your prayer. In this prayer do not quit or surrender. You are showing God in this prayer that he has no choice but to answer your prayer. At times God may delay your prayer request to test your determination, resolve and desire over your prayer request. This type of prayer works best in dire situations such as terminal illness, job loss, family violence leading to divorce and business collapse plus many other situations you may find yourself in. In whatever dire situation you find yourself in, know that our Lord God has the best plans for you because he is powerful, mighty, and loving and nothing is impossible through and by him. So long as you approach him in prayer with a sincere heart, he will be there for you. So please if you do have an adverse situation that needs you to go into this mighty prevailing prayer with the Lord, then do so without fear of its ramifications from God. This prayer is intense and with a strong passion for God to answer your prayers within the shortest time possible.

By going through these prevailing prayers with the Lord you must make sure that both your words and actions mean serious business with him. If you are faced with a dangerous situation that needs God's intervention, never be afraid to go into this heavy, intense, and prevailing prayer with the Lord. By doing this are you getting to turn things in your prayer? Here is the main verse in the bible that tells us this prayer demand.

"And there is no one who calls on Your name, who stirs himself up to take hold of You." (Isaiah 64:7)

Prayers of Thanksgiving

The shocking truth is that many people both Christians and non-Christians alike would love God to answer their prayer requests over something they need in life but when they receive, they do not come back to thank the Lord either through God's minister or directly going back to God in prayer to thank him. This is not a new thing. You can see even in the bible in the case of the ten lepers who were healed by our Lord only one came back to thank him. As you get closer to God, in your walks with him you must never forget to thank him in everything and every situation you are going through, knowing that he has answered your prayers before, and he will do the same again in the situation you want him to intervene whether it is you or on behalf of other people including your closest family members. This is what the Holy Spirit will be stirring you up to do in your walk with the Lord. It is not God who wants appreciation. Even in the ideal human society, we tend to be happy with those who acknowledge our help, who come back and appreciate us when they get what they want through our help. Why is appreciation important? Because we live in a world of problems and we must learn to appreciate those who help us today and who will help us tomorrow if we get into problems that we cannot solve and someone else intervenes.

This thankful heart must be true, real, and genuine before God when you come to him to require help or when he has already helped you and you are coming to appreciate him. Your heart must not be seen to manipulate God in your favour to get him to answer your prayers and later quit the relationship with him. Can I tell you this; he is the Lord of your heart and he even knows your thoughts before you even speak them out to him. This is where many people get into problems with God in their prayer life because they come to God with dirty hearts, thinking that God will turn a blind eye over what they are having in their life or assuming that God cannot see what is in their hearts and he will answer their prayers. This is totally wrong. God wants his children to come to him with sincere hearts with a sincere desire to be helped in their situations. I know it may be very hard sometimes if you are disappointed and hurt by other people, to have a sincere thankful heart, and that is why you must seek help from the Holy Spirit.

There is nothing God cannot do for you if you are thankful to him. When God starts to be active in your life through the Holy Spirit, he will begin to help you at your workplace, your marriage, your studies, your language, your health, your food, shelter and clothes, your income, your career, your protection, and your character. All these examples plus others will change in a twinkling of an eye. You must not only thank God for what he has done for you but also for sending his only begotten son to come and die for you to have free salvation of your soul which would have been bought at nothing to enter God's presence (heaven). We must always be grateful to our living God for reconciling us to himself through his son Jesus Christ who died on the cross to defeat the bondage of the devil on our behalf. We must always be thankful for this greater love by our Lord Jesus Christ to save us from the hands of the wicked enemy (Satan).

"Be anxious for nothing, but in everything by prayer and supplication, with thanksgiving, let your requests be made known to God; and the peace of God, which surpasses all understanding, will guard your hearts and minds through Christ Jesus." (Philippians 4:6-7).

"Speaking to one another in psalms and hymns and spiritual songs, singing and making melody in your heart to the Lord, giving thanks always for all the things to God the Father in the name of our Lord Jesus Christ" (Ephesians 5:19-20).

Pray to God the Father in the Name of Jesus

There is no other name in heaven, earth, and seas that we can access God almighty than the name of his beloved Son and our Lord Jesus Christ. It is the only name recognised by our enemy (Satan), and it makes him run away from us. Satan was disarmed on the cross by our Lord Jesus Christ, and he is no longer powerful to those who pronounced the name of Jesus Christ upon themselves. It is the only name we have access to God as all human races. It is the only name that our God the father will accept in our prayer to him if we pray through Jesus Christ name. So, when you pray using this name every hindering spirit will bow to this name and leave you in this name only.

"Let this mind be in you which was also in Christ Jesus, who, being in the form of God, did not consider it robbery to be equal with God, but made Himself of no reputation, taking the form of a bondservant, and coming in the likeness of men. And being found in appearance as a man, He humbled Himself and became obedient to the point of death, even the death of the cross. Therefore, God also has highly exalted Him and given Him the name which is above every name, that at the name of Jesus every knee should bow, of those in heaven, and of those on earth, and of those under the earth, and that every tongue should confess that Jesus Christ is Lord, to the glory of God the Father." (Philippians 2:5-11)

Listen! Jesus Christ is the only way to God. You have been set free through him. The reality is that everything in heaven, on earth and under the earth has been brought under his rulership, which you are part of if you believe in him. So, you have nothing to fear. He offered Himself as the only acceptable sacrifice to God on behalf of mankind – what a love. By accepting this reality and walk, talk, think and act by it, everything around you will change for good in your life. Simply, Christ is the Lord over all things. That is why you must pray through his name because it is the only name in which your prayers can be answered by God. There is no prayer and salvation outside the name of Jesus Christ that humankind can pray and be saved. *For there is one God and one mediator between God and humanity, the man Christ Jesus. (1 Timothy 2:5).*

His mission here on earth was to save humans who were enslaved by the devil. Christ has overcome the power of the devil and this reality must sink into your brain. There is no Satan attack on your life without your permission and there is no defeat by Satan without you not believing in the work of the cross. The only way you can be defeated by the devil is when you reject the work of the cross of Christ. Please accept and operate in this truth or the devil will intimidate you. This is the truth the devil does not want us to know. So, when you know this truth when praying to the father in the name of Jesus Christ you are sure or certain that your prayers will be answered. Jesus Christ was here to preach the message of the kingdom of God to the blinds, deaf, lame, and lowly in society. When Christ died on the Cross, he made us complete in him and in his rule demanding nothing from us in exchange for our prayers apart from praying them in his name. There was no pleasure at all for Jesus Christ to be crucified on the cross without resistance, as he was powerful and with powerful angels who could have wiped off the world in a minute. He had legions of angels, but he submitted to the cross without a fight. Think about that. He did it just for you and me. *John 3:16 says, "For God so loved the world that He gave His only begotten Son, that whoever believes in Him should not perish but have everlasting life."*

Not only Jesus Christ but all of us as human beings are of God because of God's presence in us in the form of Spirit and soul." I wish people would get this message for their soul to be saved. When Christ died on our behalves he had changed our location from the kingdom of darkness into the kingdom of his son Jesus Christ. In other words, he has removed us from the rulership of Satan to the rulership of Christ who is his son. We became children of God because of the work of the cross by Jesus Christ. Walk-in this reality and there is nothing that will stop your prayers from being answered by God.

Chapter 5

Fasting

Fasting is an important Christian spiritual ritual that must be observed by all Christians. The fact that it is also recommended by Jesus Christ in the New Testament, to all those who believed in him, makes it a necessity for those who need the move of God in their lives. Historically, fasting was also a common practice among the Jews in the Old Testament. Jesus Christ prayed and fasted and so did his disciples plus many other followers of Jesus Christ. Jesus Christ told us that prayer alone is not enough if we are to achieve a meaningful breakthrough when dealing with tough situations in our lives or in the lives of others, just as it was the case when he had healed the demon-possessed boy. His disciples were not able to cast out the demon in the boy because they did not fast. Jesus Christ also recommended to us that when we fast, we must do it in a sacred place and not open to being seen by others. He asked us to wash our faces and anoint our heads with oil as we lock ourselves into our private rooms to have private communication with God our father.

Matthew 6:16-18 says, "And when you fast, do not look gloomy like the hypocrites, for they disfigure their faces that their fasting may be seen by others. Truly, I say to you, they have received their reward. But when you fast, anoint your head and wash your face, that your fasting may not be seen by others but by your Father who is in secret. And your Father who sees in secret will reward you."

Fasting must not be seen to be a legalistic ritual, which is mandatory upon the Christian but rather should come naturally from within them if they have decided to seek God over certain matters of their lives or that of their close relatives. When you fast, note that you are putting God above everything else you do in your daily life such as your job, family, community, sports, business, politics, food, drinks, movies, television, social media, reading a book, lectures, gossiping, slandering, and the list continues. I know there may be other things you do that are not mentioned here, but even if it is so, then you must put them away or stop them at that particular time of seeking God's intervention in your situation. The reason is that you want yourself not to be distracted by other things, as this distraction itself will show God that you are not serious and mean business with him in your case. Your hunger for God more than food and drinks plus other important activities in your life show God that you truly seek him, and he will fill you up. At that isolated time for God, you will be praying and fasting, reading the bible, repenting for your sins, reading Christian books, watching Christian television channels, listening to Christian preaching, and meditating on the bible scriptures. Nothing is more or less of this during fasting if you are to have a breakthrough in your prayer request.

If fasting was relevant for Jesus Christ and his disciples, then it is still relevant today among Christians and should be observed by every single Christian if he or she is to make progress in their walk with Christ. There are many types of fasting mentioned in the bible and which were practised in different situations by different individuals, bringing about a turnaround of their adverse situations by God.

The Importance of Fasting

The most important reason for fasting is to seek God's attention with all your full heart and mind. The reasons we fast include but are not limited to, the following seeking Holy Spirit guidance, seeking spiritual growth, seeking intimacy with God, seeking repentance, seeking freedom, and seeking humility. It is all about putting everything else you do aside for God. It is also indicating to God how you are serious about his knowledge and your walk with him. God promised us abundant life on earth and there is nowhere you can receive this other than to seek God through fasting which gives you the power to dominate all things on earth. In your Christian faith, fasting is where the power to live an abundant life on earth is, and the strength you need to continue to fight more spiritual battles ahead of you. If our Lord Jesus Christ fasted when he was here on earth, then we have no choice but to also fast.

Matthew 4:2- *"And when He had fasted forty days and forty nights, afterwards He was hungry."*

We must fast when everything around us looks desperate and hopeless, both spiritually and physically for God's intervention. When your life is in danger and you are not sure of a way out then you must fast to seek God's intervention. The reason you seek God is this, that nothing comes your way without his full knowledge, but not only that there is nothing impossible through him. So, when you fast you are seeking his power to intervene in your situation. The problem you are facing is an invitation from him to seek him through prayer and fasting. We live in a very dangerous world full of natural disasters, wars, human hatred, death, starvation, family breakdown and sickness that needs you to draw near to God every day in prayers and fasting for spiritual breakthrough in your conditions and for your protection as well.

If we want to maintain our close relationship with God then we must not only fast when we are in desperate situations, but even when we are happy. A good relationship cannot be sustained or maintained just when there is a need, but rather through daily communication, and one of the strong ways we communicate with God our Father is through prayer and fasting. Fasting supernaturally draws you to God through humility in your heart. In fasting, we humble ourselves before the Father to hear our voices and to answer our prayers. Through a fast, we humble ourselves by getting our thoughts off ourselves in our daily routines such as eating our favourite foods and drinks but also abstaining from our close friends for God. The rewards from him for fasting are enormous ranging from spiritual and physical healing, a closer walk with him and more importantly peace when everything around us looks bad. If we want to see the power of God in us and to work actively through us, then we must fast in order to live an abundant life here on earth. Below you can look at what fasting does not only to individuals but also nations when they seek God's intervention spiritually.

"Then the people of Nineveh believed in God, and they called a fast and put on sackcloth from the greatest to the least of them. When the word reached the king of Nineveh, he arose from his throne, laid aside his robe from him, covered himself with sackcloth and sat on the ashes. He issued a proclamation and it said, "In Nineveh by the decree of the king and his nobles: Do not let man, beast, herd, or flock taste a thing. Do not let them eat or drink water. But both man and beast must be covered with sackcloth, and let men call on God earnestly that each may turn from his wicked way and from the violence which is in his hands. Who knows, God may turn and relent and withdraw His burning anger so that we will not perish. Then God saw their works, that they turned from their evil way; and God relented from the disaster that He had said He would bring upon them, and He did not do it." (Jonah 3:5-10)

2 Chronicles 7:14-15 says, "if My people who are called by My name will humble themselves, and pray and seek My face, and turn from their wicked ways, then I will hear from heaven, and will forgive their sin and heal their land. "Now My eyes will be open and My ears attentive to prayer made in this place."

Psalm 35:13-14 – "I wore sackcloth; I afflicted myself with fasting; I prayed with head bowed on my chest. I went about as though I grieved for my friend or my brother; as one who laments his mother, I bowed down in mourning."

When we fast, we are also seeking God's intervention in certain strongholds areas in our lives where the devil has gotten hold of us. There are things that we can never get rid of until God himself helps us. These are called addictions by the world, yet the bible refers to them as devil strongholds. When you get addicted to certain lifestyles or habits you can never get rid of alone then know that there are demons behind them, that will never let you go from them. We fast to break off our life's strongholds of addictions such as alcohol, drug abuse, smoking, adultery, pornography, fornication, cheating, gossip, slander, and even social media addiction. Fasting can free us from the bondage of wickedness (sins) and break off every yoke (addictions).

God warned us through prophet Isaiah, that when we fast, we must avoid all the devil's traps. Because we know that when we are hungry, our tempers flare up easily and our anger erupts so easily towards others who may be around us. During our fasting we must not think, speak and act harshly to our neighbours or else we risk not receiving our breakthrough from God. God wants us not to quarrel or fight when we are fasting or to deny the poor a helping hand if we are fasting or else, he will not answer our prayers. Instead, he wants us to share our food with the hungry, our house with the homeless and our clothes with the naked.

Isaiah 58:3-7 "Why have we fasted, and you see it not? Why have we humbled ourselves, and you take no knowledge of it?' Behold, in the day of your fast you seek your own pleasure and oppress all your workers. Behold, you fast only to quarrel and to fight and to hit with a wicked fist. Fasting like yours this day will not make your voice to be heard on high. Is such the fast that I choose, a day for a person to humble himself? Is it to bow down his head like a reed, and to spread sackcloth and ashes under him? Will you call this a fast, and a day acceptable to the Lord? "Is not this the fast that I choose: to loose the bonds of wickedness, to undo the straps of the yoke, to let the oppressed go free, and to break every yoke? Is it not to share your bread with the hungry and bring the homeless poor into your house; when you see the naked, to cover him and not to hide yourself from your own flesh?"

Types of Fasting

The Complete Forty (40), Days Fast Without Both Food and Water

This type of fasting was only done by two people in the bible namely, Jesus Christ and Moses. This is one of the dangerous fasts that I have not done, but, who knows, I may do it in future because with the Lord all things are possible. The reason why I give myself as an example here is that you must consider it carefully as it may be fatal if you have no strong relationship with God. The above-mentioned people did it because they had a strong relationship with God. I am not suggesting in any way that it cannot be done, all I am saying is that one must be cautious when doing this type of fasting in order for it not to turn into a catastrophe or tragedy. As far as I am concerned, I know one great man of God called Dr Myles Munroe, who once said in one of the sermons that he had done it easily and without side effects at all. I am not suggesting in any way in this book that you should do this fasting according to my recommendation, but rather as one of the important fasts that Christians may practice. You must consider all prevailing conditions in your life if you are to do this fast including your health conditions.

"So he was there with the Lord forty days and forty nights; he did not eat bread or drink water. And he wrote on the tablets the words of the covenant, the Ten Commandments" (Exodus 34:28 NASB).

"And after He had fasted forty days and forty nights, He then became hungry" (Matthew 4:2).

Normal Complete Fast

This is a fast that can last half a day or the whole day, several days, weeks or even a month for some people. This is a common fast in many scriptures of the bible. Perhaps, if one wants to do forty days fasting, then you must start with this fasting as one moves up gradually to the forty days fasting. As the saying goes, you must start somewhere to end up somewhere.

"Go, assemble all the Jews who are found in Susa, and fast for me; do not eat or drink for three days, night or day. I and my maidens also will fast in the same way. And thus I will go into the king, which is not according to the law; and if I perish, I perish" (Esther 4:16).

"Yet even now," declares the Lord, "Return to Me with all your heart, and with fasting, weeping and mourning" (Joel 2:12).

"Then I proclaimed a fast there at the river of Ahava, that we might humble ourselves before our God to seek from Him a safe journey for us, our little ones, and all our possessions. For I was ashamed to request from the king troops and horsemen to protect us from the enemy on the way, because we had said to the king, "The hand of our God is favourably disposed to all those who seek Him, but His power and His anger are against all those who forsake Him." So we fasted and sought our God concerning this matter, and He listened to our entreaty" (Ezra 8:21-23).

A Partial Fast

This fast is also known as a 3-day spiritual fast. The basic idea of this fast is to abstain from delicious, tasty food for a loose kind of tasteless food if you like. There is nowhere in the bible where this kind of fasting can be found other than in Daniel 10. In this fast, you must avoid meat, tasty bread, wine and no body lotion or perfume and instead eat fruits, vegetables, and water for 21 days. What this fast carry in it, is the fact that you humble yourself before God by avoiding a luxurious eating style or habit.

I did not eat any tasty food, nor did meat or wine enter my mouth, nor did I use any ointment at all until the entire three weeks were completed" (Daniel 10:3).

"So I gave my attention to the Lord God to seek Him by prayer and supplications, with fasting, sackcloth and ashes" (Daniel 9:3).

"Please test your servants for ten days and let us be given some vegetables to eat and water to drink" (Daniel 1:12).

Other Types of Fast

These types of fasts are non-food such as; abstaining from sexual intercourse between husband and wife, abstaining from social media and other forms of communications and information and focussing on the bible only, and finally abstaining from drinking water and alcohol for periods of time. This can be one day, three days, seven days or more to seek the face of the Lord only. Again, is entirely dependent upon you and the situation you are in to be able to do these types of fasts. Everything depends on how hungry and thirsty you are for God's knowledge. These types of fasts are also supported by the bible in the following scriptures:

I did not eat any tasty food, nor did meat or wine enter my mouth, nor did I use any ointment at all until the entire three weeks were completed" (Daniel 10:3).

"So I gave my attention to the Lord God to seek Him by prayer and supplications, with fasting, sackcloth and ashes" (Daniel 9:3).

"Stop depriving one another, except by agreement for a time, so that you may devote yourselves to prayer, and come together again so that Satan will not tempt you because of your lack of self-control" (1 Corinthians 7:5).

"He said to the people, "Be ready for the third day; do not go near a woman" (Exodus 19:15).

Chapter 6

The Shield of Faith

The Roman soldiers' shields were 1.2 meters long and 0.76 meters wide. These shields were big enough to cover the whole bodies of soldiers while being targeted by the arrows of the enemy. They were offensive as well as defensive weapons of war. The Roman soldiers had every confidence in their well-designed and well-built shields that could bring down all the fiery darts and arrows of their enemy. The shields were made of animal hides woven together that were almost as strong as steel. Their shields were tough, durable, stronger, and lasted for all seasons of war. Because the shields were made of leather skins, every soldier had the responsibility to maintain the shield using oil to keep it soft, supple, and pliable. A soldier needed to keep his shield in good condition with the daily oil rub on the shield to keep in shape. With confidence in their shields, Roman soldiers did not doubt in their minds that winning the battle was a non-negotiable thing but a must. Before the soldiers went into battle the victory was already determined by their shields and their confidence in them, and that the enemy's shields were no match to theirs. So, they went to war knowing that they would win the war and they did. As a matter of fact, the predetermined outcome about the war they had in their minds was not changed by the actual war and so they had to prevail.

FIGHTING THE INVISIBLE ENEMY

The Shield of Faith

In addition to all this, take up the shield of faith, with which you can extinguish all the flaming arrows of the evil one. —Ephesians 6:16

Made from goat-skin or calf skin stretched over sturdy pieces of wood, the Roman shield stood four feet long and was three-feet wide. Iron rims were fitted along the top and bottom edges, and an iron circle was attached to the center of the shield. The boards curved inward and a leather strap was fastened to the shield's back.

Before going into battle, Roman soldiers drenched their leather-covered shields with water. When the fiery arrows of their enemies struck these soaked shields, the flames were immediately extinguished. Soldiers could put their shields together and have more protection.

The shield of faith is the Christian's protection against temptation. Whenever we trust that God will provide everything we need, "the spiritual forces of evil" cannot tempt us with the lie that sin can provide a better life than God will. Ephesians 6:12

In this way, "all the flaming arrows of the evil one"—every temptation and distraction that Satan may hurl at God's people—can be stopped. Ephesians 6:16

When faced with authentic faith in God, the powers of darkness are overcome. That is why the apostle John could say, "This is the victory that has overcome the world, even our faith." 1 John 5:4

As for God, his way is perfect, He is a shield for all who take refuge in him —2 Samuel 22:31
My shield is God Most High, who saves the upright in heart. —Psalm 7:10
He has prepared his deadly weapons; he makes ready his flaming arrows. —Psalm 7:13
You give me your shield of victory, and your right hand sustains me. —Psalm 18:35
Also Genesis 15:1; Psalm 3:3; 18:2; 28:7; 33:20; 46:9; 76:3

thyreos—shield or door
scutum—shield

Source: https://www.christianbook.com

St. Paul refers to our faith in God as Christians to that of the Roman soldiers' faith in their shield. In other words, our Faith in God equals the faith of Roman soldiers in their shields during the war. Our faith in God should be the source of our hope of protection in life as we go through every difficult moment of our lives. No matter what comes your way in this life whether it is the lack of employment, sickness, divorce, job loss, infertility, natural disasters, starvation, poverty, violence, wars and so forth, we must trust God to lead us through all of these for the better outcomes. We must trust God daily as the source of our protection just as the Roman soldiers had to trust their shields as the source of their protection and they had to look after them daily so that they would not become hard, brittle, and stiff as if they were not cared for. We must allow the Holy Spirit to lead us in our faith, for our faith to be refreshed daily.

What we know is that faith does move God and get us to access what God has in store for us if we believe in him. When our faith is grounded and rooted in things of God – the Bible, the Holy Spirit, Jesus Christ, and God the Father, as the sources of our truth, then nothing can easily bring us down in this world. Apart from these sources, nothing else can save us from the dangers we face here on earth daily. It is our faith in these sources that will extinguish all the fiery darts and arrows of the devil, just as the Roman soldiers while going into the battle, dipped their shields in the water to snuff all the arrows directed at them by the enemy. The only thing that will quench the arrows of the devil is our faith in God, not in the medical field and governments, who are trying to provide alternative solutions to our problems. God is the only source of solution that does not fail us.

"Without Faith, You Cannot Please God"

The world walks by sight and the believers (Christians) walks by faith. The only way we can access God is by faith. Furthermore, the only way we can access our blessings from God is by faith. God is a spirit, and we cannot see the spirit with our own naked eyes. Although we are spirits as humans, we have a body that hinders our spiritual eyes from seeing spiritual things or other spirits. What activates our spirit part of us is faith in God, but also when we allow the spirit of God to live in us to connect us with God who is a spirit. Hence, the spirits do see us, but we do not see the spirits so long as we are in the body – it is only when we die and leave the body that our spirits will see other spirits including God. The only way we can see spirits is through faith believing that spirits do exist including God, who is a spirit.

It is by faith believing that the spirits do exist, and they can communicate to us, that warrant the spirits to speak to us (mankind). The faith that is grounded on the things of God extinguishes all the arrows directed against us by the dark kingdom. The only way you can defeat Satan is to have unwavering faith in God. The idea in your mind and heart that God will prevail against all the attacks by Satan keep you going as it gives you hope for the future. The first spirit that will have an encounter with us if we believe and are baptized by it, is the Holy Spirit of God. It is this spirit (Holy Spirit) who connects us to the other spirits namely, Jesus Christ and God almighty. Faith is an offensive weapon that will shield you off on the fiery darts of the wicked on.

St. Paul referred to faith in God as the shield of faith because in war shield protects your important organs of the body such as heart, kidneys, eyes, and stomach. The shield can be used to protect any other parts of the body depending on how the person used it. Without faith, we cannot appeal to God. We are to take the shield of faith. Faith is a complete trust and dependence on God in all ways and for all things. It is an unwavering confidence in Jesus Christ. Faith in Jesus Christ (your shield) puts "Him" between you and the enemy. It is written in **Genesis 15:1 that the Lord said, "Fear not, Abram: I am thy shield"**. "The Lord, the shield of thy help"-Deuteronomy 33:29. The shield of victory – 2 Samuel 22:36 Niv. The shield of faith is faith in the Lord. Through faith, all things can be overcome. Whatever the devil brings against you, believe that God is there, and he is willing to help you. Whether it is sickness, family problems, childlessness, depression, stress, or financial difficulty, God will set you free from all of them. Have unwavering faith in God at the weakest point of your life and you will witness God move.

We cannot understand faith until we have broken it down and discussed it in detail. Faith according to the book of **Hebrews 11:1: "Now faith is the substance of things hoped for, the evidence of things not seen."** So, let us look at the keyword there – "substance" – that "faith is the substance" of things hoped for. If we take the word substance as it is then it will mean "Spiritual substance" inside every single person created by God. However, there are some other bible scholars and other people of faith who do not agree with the interpretations of the word substance as it is, because of its meaning in other languages of its translation such as Greek. The word Substance in the Greek language is "hypostasis," which means the following: assurance, confidence, confident expectations, a setting under or support or an assured impression. So, the definition of faith from first or second interpretation will be something like this; the assurance of things hoped for, Confident attitude toward God, reliance, and trustworthiness towards God. Whichever the case, faith is the substance/assurance of things we hoped for that is inside of us. It is the confidence we have inside of us that things will happen the way we would love them to happen regardless of the challenges we faced inside/outside us.

We have already seen faith as something within us and the fundamental question we should ask ourselves is this: who deposited this substance within us? And the answer would be our Creator (God). As a matter of fact, we are created by God-knowing almost a lot of things about him and his other creations than we think or deny. When we are born, we are born with the curiosity to know how everything within us and around us came together to be as it is or as they are. Conversely, God has already given us a measure of faith in his creations including ourselves (humankind). If he had not done this then we would have had difficulty in knowing that he exists and that we can be saved through his son Jesus Christ. The bible teaches us that we are saved by grace through faith in Jesus Christ. It is only through faith that we can qualify for God grace.

When we have this measure of faith already deposited into us by God, we can grow it to a much higher level through the Holy Spirit by reading the bible and activating our prayer life. St. Paul put this very well in the book of Romans 10:17- **"So then faith comes by hearing and hearing by the word of God."** This verse indicates that your faith in God can grow to a higher (or greater) level by reading and studying the word of God. If you can commit a great deal of time to read the bible, the Holy Spirit will help you increase your knowledge through deep revelations and understanding of the verses. Your knowledge will begin to increase inside of you towards the things of God – an increasing explosive appetite to know God a lot more. Not only will you begin to know God, but you will also begin to know Jesus Christ and the Holy Spirit better, but not only that, but you will also begin to develop a one-on-one relationship with the Holy Spirit as your first contact for launching deeply into things of God. You will begin to hear and discern the voice of the Holy Spirit clearly. Your wisdom and word of knowledge about things of God will start to grow rapidly. This only happens when you are hungry for things of God, but when you begin to slow down, your level of faith will also begin to slow down. This means that your level of faith corresponds to the level of your commitment to the things of God.

The bible tells us that God through the help of the Holy Spirit wants to increase our knowledge of him. And the only way we can know God better is by reading his word, the bible. If you are willing to increase your level of knowledge about God through studying of scriptures, then the spirit of God will supernaturally increase your level of faith in things of God. Nothing disappoints God almighty more than the people who die because of a lack of knowledge of him. Once your level of faith begins to increase over time in the knowledge of God then he can trust you, and he is able to do great things for you or through for others. Believe me, there are correlations between you doing your bit and God doing his bit. This can be summed up in this simple statement: as you grow in the knowledge of God your level of faith starts to increase with it. Isn't that beautiful to work for and with the Lord of the universe?

This brings us to another important part of faith. Work!!! As it is popularly known "faith without works is dead." Yes, it is true that we can be saved by grace through our faith but that does not mean that the work has no important role to play in your walk of salvation. Please observe this statement with your full attention: your faith in God remains a claim until it is tested. It is one thing to claim that you have faith in God when things are perfectly okay with you, but it is another thing to prove that you have faith in God when things are not okay with you. For example, it is easy to believe that God can heal others when they are sick of a life-threatening disease such as cancer, but it is another thing to believe that God can heal you when you are sick with the same life-threatening disease such as cancer. What you do for God is what will truly prove that you have faith in God. For instance, Abraham, our father of faith, proved himself to God when he was willing to sacrifice his son for God when asked to do so. So, Abraham became the true father of faith through his willingness to sacrifice his own son to God. This argument is correctly summed up in the book of ***James 2:17,21,22,24-26: "Thus also faith by itself, if it does not have works, is dead ... Was not Abraham our father justified by works when he offered Isaac his son on the altar? Do you see that faith was working together with his works, and by works, faith was made perfect? ... You see then that a man is justified by works, and not by faith only ... For as the body without the spirit is dead, so faith without works is dead also."***

These verses indicate that faith alone without work will never get a job done for God. Work is there to back-up your faith in God. Once you become a born-again Christian you can now work for God. When he begins to instruct you to do a specific job for him then you must be able to do it for him or else your faith will be considered dead by God.

Furthermore, when you have faith mixed with work then God can trust you and you can trust God. A mutual relationship is developed between you and God. When this relationship is developed and is working then it is fair to say that at this moment you can walk by faith but not sight as the world does. What this means is that we can now do what the Lord tells us, not what we see happening in the world. For instance, if the economies of the world are crushing the way they are now due to Coronavirus, the fear of people losing their jobs and thus, in turn, losing their houses will grip them, but when you put your trust in God you will never be worried as he is in full control of your life. Hence when you have fully surrendered your life to God then you must not be worried about what this world throws at you as God is in full control of your life. The point I am trying to put across is that your life is now a life of faith in God – not a life of faith in yourself, parents, colleagues, friends, finances, investment shares, and bosses.

The complete surrendering of our lives to God would mean that no matter what comes our ways, we have the unwavering faith that God is in control and he will turn it around for our favour. Sometimes in life, we have a high level of faith in God when nothing has happened to us, but when nasty storms begin to hit us, that level of faith in God will come down crashing. That is why we must not take our eyes off Jesus Christ as the author and finisher of our faith. This was exactly the case with Peter as he was able to walk on water looking steadfastly at Jesus Christ but as soon as he began to look at the storm, then his faith fell, and he began to sink. I am now convinced that we must leave everything in the hands of God and let him work out our problems instead of constantly worrying about them. For with God, nothing is impossible. Once you know that God is the Lord of all things, both visible and invisible, then you should be able to relax and put your full trust and faith in him; no matter what the situation looks like, he will turn it around for you.

Contrastingly, this is what breaks the camel's back for the devil: you must trust the Lord until the point of death. The devil will scare you off to the point of death, but if you know it is only God who has the keys to death, then he will quickly back off. You must know that Jesus Christ descended to the lower part of the earth to get keys of death off the devil. And since then, the devil is disarmed and powerless for those who have and who will believe in Jesus Christ. You must know that Jesus Christ is the Lord of all things – both living and dead things. That is how powerful your faith should be in the Lord. But having said that you must also fight a good fight of faith. There are four key statements you must always have at your fingertips in this life as you walk with God: be faithful until death, continue in the faith grounded and steadfast, fight the good fight of faith and be brave and strong trusting in the Lord that he will never let you down.

Nevertheless, you must not lose your faith in God no matter what is happening to you here on earth. Once you have developed a personal relationship with the Holy Spirit and thereafter with our Lord Jesus Christ then there is no reason at all to lose your faith in him. To that effect you keep your level of faith up in God on earth then there is no reason you should not fulfil all your divine assignments here on earth and eventually have your heavenly salvation afterwards. We must make the Holy Spirit our true friend or else there is no way we can prosper in what we do here on earth. That is why when Christians have this fact in their minds and in their hearts, they will have strong faith in God and will never turn away from him until death. The word of God will give you extraordinary knowledge that will keep you going in him until death. Once you begin to experience the supernatural power of God in your life then life becomes simpler and less worrisome for you, knowing that he is the master of your life. All things will work together for you all the time, whether good or bad. Faith is the only way you can walk with God in this life. It is the supernatural modus-operandi.

Chapter 7

The Belt of Truth

St. Paul compared the truth to the belt worn by the Roman soldiers around their waist, while in the battle against their enemies of other nations. Part of what made the Roman soldiers powerful and well equipped for the battle were the belts used to tie up and hold in place tightly the garments and other weapons of war, so they would not get in the way while fighting in battle. These belts were designed to last long for every season and acted as the first protective equipment that clung closely to the soldiers shielding the most vulnerable parts of the soldier's bodies. The belts gave the Roman soldiers every confidence in mobility and defence while fighting in the battle. The belts were (among others), some of the things that removed the fear equation in the battle from the Roman soldiers. The Roman soldiers trusted in their belts over those of their enemies giving them the confidence of victory in the battle over their enemies. The Roman emperor lasted long enough on earth partly because of these well-designed belts. Even in our world today, the nations' armies' belts continue to play an important role in holding up their trousers, also needed to tuck in their shirts and hold in place everything they wear on their bodies. So, without a doubt, belts are still an important part of the soldiers' lives in the army today.

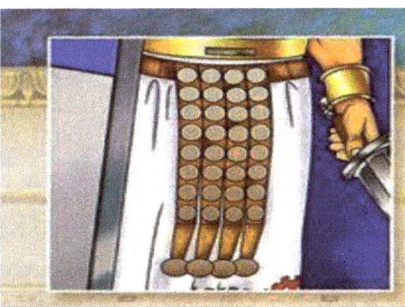

The Belt of Truth

With the belt of truth buckled around your waist —Ephesians 6:14

Description of Armor	The "belt of truth" was named after the leather belt with an apron that hung in front of the Roman soldier's groin and lower abdomen. Small brass plates were attached to the apron to provide the greatest possible protection.
Historical Background	When preparing for battle, the belt would have been the first piece of protective equipment put on by a soldier. It clung closely to the soldier and shielded some of the most vulnerable areas of his body.
Application	The belt prepares one to be ready for action. Belts were used to tie up the garments so they would not get in the way while fighting. The call to have "your loins girt about with truth" is a call to *be prepared*. Christians always need to be ready to defend themselves against the powers of darkness and not be caught unaware. You can be prepared in every circumstance, by making certain that you are a person of truth. This includes— • Knowing the good news about Jesus and explaining why you believe in him. • Living as a person of integrity—as someone who is honest and trustworthy. *Live such good lives . . . that, though they accuse you of doing wrong, they may see your good deeds and glorify God . . .* —1 Peter 2:12
Other Biblical Passages	*Always be prepared to give an answer to everyone who asks you to give the reason for the hope that you have. But do this with gentleness and respect . . .* —1 Peter 3:15, 16 *For God so loved the world that he gave his one and only Son, that whoever believes in him shall not perish but have eternal life.* —John 3:16
Greek or Latin Term	*cinculum militaire*—a leather belt

Source: https://www.christianbook.com

As Christians, the reason why St. Paul had to refer to the truth as the belt for our spiritual warfare, is the fact that truth stabilises things and holds things in the proper place and proper order. The first wardrobe the living God has given us to put on and to wear permanently on us, as we fight the spiritual warfare is the **"truth"** like that belt on the waist of the Roman soldier. Truth is important in this flawed world where there is no longer what is collectively viewed and accepted as one solid truth for everybody. We live in a world today where my truth is not your truth and your neighbour's truth may not be your truth. This is so fatal if there is nothing believed by almost everyone as truth then we do not have the truth. If we do not have the truth, then we do not have the direction for ourselves and our human society. So, you can see how dangerous it can get if we do not believe in one truth and stand up for that one truth. Imagine a human society in which everyone does and believes what is right in their own eyes.

Alternatively, as well Christians need to know that there is an enemy of truth, who twists and distorts the truth with lies. All of us are born not as liars, but we become liars as we grow up and live on earth. Why is this? Because we have Satan, whom we found on earth and we will leave on earth, being the one who creates chaos and disorder so that everything he wants us to believe and do is a lie. The bible is very clear in this that Satan is the father of lies and there is no truth in him. ***"You are of your father the devil, and the desires of your father you want to do. He was a murderer from the beginning and does not stand in the truth, because there is no truth in him. When he speaks a lie, he speaks from his own resources, for he is a liar and the father of it. John 8:44. NKJV.*** On many occasions, people in their own hearts know what the truth of any matter is in every situation, yet they continue to lie against the truth to protect themselves from others because of their wrongdoings. Instead of accepting the truth of what we have done, we lie to cover up the wrong to escape the penalty for our wrongdoings. Almost in everything we do, we are proud when we do it right but ashamed when we do it wrong. So, when we feel ashamed of what we have done, we lie to protect our reputation from others.

The reason why the world is a mess today is that we do what we think is right by us and for us. But little do we know that what we do is influenced by Satan. When we speak lies, know that we are speaking from the position of the master of lies, who is Satan. Every time we depart from the truth of God, then we must also know that we are venturing into the demonic territory where our thoughts and our actions can be infiltrated with lies. The bible tells that if everyone was to accept their mistakes and be ready to face the consequences of their mistakes, then we would never have liars and for that matter, Satan would never have ground in our lives.

As Christians, we have an obligation from God to fight the lie with the truth. Know that God is the truth and everything from him is the truth, whereas on the other hand lying is from the devil and the devil is the liar and the father of all lies. When every Christian believes God is the source of truth and does everything from that point of view, everything around him is completely stabilised and in order. Where there is truth, there is clarity and victory versus where there is lie there is confusion and defeat.

When you speak the truth, know that Jesus Christ is the master of all truth, and when you speak lies, know that Satan is the master of all lies. It is only when you know the true source of the truth, that the truth can set you free.

The world today continues to struggle to know what really the truth is. How to say the truth and how to maintain the truth. The truth of the matter is that we must accept the truth internally for it to manifest externally. The only way we can walk in the truth is to allow the truth to live inside of us. Truth must be seen in what we do, speak and think. The only way people can believe you as a truth-teller is to allow the truth to rule in your decision-making process and the choices you make in life. I may ask you today, what is the truth according to you? And I will imagine your answers to be along these lines: truth is what I believe to be real to me; that the truth is what others agree with me, say, and believe to be true, and that the truth is the facts-based principles supported by evidence over a matter, situation, or thing. These definitions as to what the truth is, plus other answers you could give me, do make sense and have elements of reality in them as to what really is the truth. Yes, these definitions are partly correct, but they are not the true definition of what the truth is.

Building internal truth is important to Christian. Everything you do must be based on nothing but the truth of God. Being honest with what we do, speak, and think in our minds must be the basis of building on the truth inside of us. Our desires, motives, beliefs, and mistakes must be based on the truth. When we are wrong, we must admit that we are wrong and apologise to the people offended by our actions. God already knows everything about us and there is no reason to hide our mistakes from him. In fact, the reason why we do not receive from God when we go into prayer with him- is because we are not honest in our motives with him.

We try to hide our sins from him. Listen to me God will never turn a blind eye on your sins to grant you what you are trying to access through prayer until you have done with your own sins and have forgiven other people their sins. For example, we hold people in our hearts as our enemies and go to God in prayer to forgive our sins thinking that he is not aware of our problems with other people.

Interestingly as well, these definitions of what is the truth are also undermined or devalued by these sayings; what is true to you may not be true to me, and there is no such thing as right or wrong answer (meaning there no true one collective definition of truth.) Sometimes people who would want to know what the truth is really begun to ponder and ask a question; what then is the truth? if it can be watered-down like this!!! I want you to know today that you are not alone. I was once in this state of confusion to define the truth. But today I have good news for you as to what is the true definition of the truth. This is all happening now especially at our time so that many people can be deceived by the devil. The idea is to get you to believe that there no such thing as wrong or right. This is a very dangerous assertion. We all know that there is something wrong when we do not do the right thing by ourselves and by others.

Here is the true definition of the truth. Truth is a "spiritual being" who stays in you and enables you to believe, speak and maintain the truth. Truth is a person. Truth is Jesus Christ. Jesus Christ said ***John 14:6-I am the truth***. When Jesus Christ is in you the truth is in you. Truth is a strong weapon of your defence against the lies or deception directed at you by Satan. Truth becomes your standing ground against all lies when you know and believe that there is the Holy Spirit-Jesus Christ and God almighty. Truth also becomes your standing ground when you believe what the bibles say about the origin of all things (both living and nonliving). With these in mind, you can liberate yourself from all the lies in the world today. If you are Christian, you must admit the fact that Jesus Christ is the truth, and you will not be deceived or struggle to tell the truth and stand up for the truth. When you receive new information contradicting this fact then you must always dismiss it by referring to the bible as the source of your truth. Jesus Christ said, ***John 17:17-Sanctify them by your truth***. Your word (the bible) is the truth. If the opportunity presents itself to you which compromised this fact, then you must avoid it. You must have this rule of thumb, if it is the truth, I will join it and defend it, but if it is a lie then I will get out of it and not defend it. Truth must be the first line of your defence against the devil. Truth is to govern the struggle we are in. Standing in Jesus must be based on the truth. It must be based on being founded and built upon "the rock" (Jesus).

The alternative to the truth lies in another spiritual being. What causes us to hurt, desire, hate, doubt, fear and not to forgive among others is a spirit called Satan. All these plus others come from him and they are all lies. They may sound like truth, but counterfeits presented to you to deceive you and to block your blessing from God. I also want you to know that lie is a spiritual being. When this spiritual being is in you, he enables you to speak the lies, defend the lies and struggle to tell the truth because there is no truth in him according to Jesus Christ. This liar is Satan. Have you wondered why some of us are born liars? It is because we are born in the sin of this spirit who had deceived our fathers and our great grandfathers including Adam. He has been lying and he has lied from the beginning of creation according to the bible. As he did to Adam and Eve, in the Garden of Eden, he will also do the same to you today by giving you twisted information-half-truth and half-lie. Because he knows if he had to give you a complete lie you will discover it straight away and avoid it. For example, he will not tell you to go and kill a person, so he builds anger within you that turns into a rage that enables you to kill the person. The bible says when the devil speaks lies he speaks from his nature because he is the father of all lies. ***(John 8:44). Lying is the main problem today in the world as people try to defend themselves from their mistakes through lies. I want you to know from today that lying is what Satan will use to keep you in bondage***. Keep away from lie and you will be free. The only way you can get rid of this spirit in you is by accepting Jesus Christ is the truth.

Power of the new information: it is only when you know the true source of the truth, that you can be "set free." It is only when you do this, that you can know the truth and speak the truth in your day-to-day life. Without this, you will struggle to do the right thing in life.

Say the truth and the truth will set you free. Jesus Christ is the truth. Let him live in you and you will never struggle to say the truth. It is not a choice; it is a must-do if you are a Christian. When you come to Christ as a Christian, you must decrease as Christ increases in you (humble yourself as you die to yourself and Christ takes over). It is not a joke; you are either Christian or not a Christian at all. When Christ takes over your life, he must dominate what you think, speak, and do. Without these, you are not a Christian. It sounds harsh but a reality if you want God to change your life for good. Things of the body such as the lust of the flesh, lust of the eye and the pride of life must all be crucified. For a simple reason, God resists the proud and self-centred people, and they will never see him. Doing one's own will must decrease and doing God's will must increase. Being loyal and obedient to God's demands and requirements must increase. The love for oneself, including obeying people above God, must decrease as the love of God increases in your life. When Christ dominates your life, it must be seen in areas such as; reading and believing the bible as the true word of God, helping people in need, praying and fasting and leading a repentant lifestyle. If you have done all of these you will see the seven seals of God manifesting in you as namely: power, wealth, wisdom, strength, honour, glory, and blessings. Christ is the truth; you better believe this before it is too late.

Chapter 8

The Breastplate of Righteousness

Breastplates were important protective equipment fastened by the Roman soldiers around their chests to protect their important organs such as hearts and lungs from the enemy arrows. As you can see from the above picture the breastplates were vest-like types of equipment made of metal rings put together to form solid chainmail. When Roman soldiers were dressed in their breastplates, they had every confidence that they were well protected, and as they went to war, they had complete assurance that they would win the battle. They were very confident that there were no other kingdoms on earth who could design the pieces of equipment of war like the Roman emperor. Not only were the breastplates weapons of protection, but they were also sources of beauty. They were made of bright and shiny golden brass, which, when the soldier moved backwards, their shoulders could turn into blinding glare that could blind their opponent's eyes as the fighting continued. They were offensive and defensive weapons of war.

The Breastplate of Righteousness

With the breastplate of righteousness in place —Ephesians 6:14

The Roman soldier would have fastened the breastplate around his chest.[1] There were two types of breastplates. The first type of breastplate was fashioned by joining several broad, curved metal bands together using leather thongs. The other was a type of chain mail, constructed by linking small metal rings together until they formed a vest.

The purpose of both types of armor was the same—to protect the soldier's vital organs. If a soldier failed to wear his breastplate, an arrow could easily reach a soldier's chest, piercing his heart or lungs.

In Isaiah 59, the LORD puts on "righteousness as a breastplate," and goes to battle against injustice and corruption, restoring peace and order to the land.

God offers his own righteousness to every believer in Jesus Christ. Righteousness is not something that anyone can gain by doing good deeds. It comes from faith in Jesus Christ. Titus 3:5; Philippians 3:9

Putting on the breastplate of righteousness means—
- Believing in Jesus and his righteousness, not our own. Galatians 2:20, 21
- Standing firm against injustice and corruption. Leviticus 19:15, Hebrews 1:9
- Knowing that God promises his protection against the forces of evil for those who have faith in Jesus. 2 Thessalonians 3:3

Breastplate (chainmail)

[The LORD'S] own arm worked salvation for him, and his own righteousness sustained him. He put on righteousness as his breastplate. —Isaiah 59:16, 17
For in the gospel a righteousness from God is revealed, a righteousness that is by faith from first to last, just as it is written: "The righteous will live by faith." —Romans 1:17
This righteousness from God comes through faith in Jesus Christ to all who believe. —Romans 3:22

lorica segmentata—breastplate with metal bands
lorica hamata—chainmail breastplate

Source: https://www.christianbook.com

As Christians the weapon of war we must wear around our chests all the time is righteousness. Righteousness is a weapon of war because we have an enemy (Satan) that wants to attack our important organs of faith- our spirits and souls. Satan daily wants to penetrate the minds and emotions of Christians who do not do the right thing and as a result, miss the mark of the righteousness of God. Every day Satan will whisper in the ears of believers that God will never heal their sickness, they will never be rich while serving God, God is not watching them as they commit adultery, God will never accept them back to him because of their sins and so forth. These are all his lies he wants you to believe in order to pull you away from your God protection zone.

If you do not have your breastplate on, you can be easily destroyed by the devil with his lies. He will try to convince you in your mind by bombarding you with many wrong thoughts and try to pressurise you through your emotions so you will quit trusting and believing God at the difficult moments of your life. When you have the truth and act on that truth, then you cannot be easily shaken by Satan. You must be formally established in your God-given righteousness to win against the devil's accusations every time you are in trouble. When Christians know that they are in righteousness they can pray to God with full authority and power and their prayers can be answered. The bible is very clear on this one: **"For He made Him who knew no sin to be sin for us, that we might become the righteousness of God in Him." 2 Corinthians 5:21. NKJV.**

In the verse above we are standing on the righteousness of God. Because "none of us is righteous before God". If it were because of our own righteousness none of us would have been saved by God. We stand on the righteousness of our Lord Jesus Christ.

The breastplate of righteousness is the strong weapon of your spiritual warfare against the devil. Righteousness is the perfect holiness of Jesus Christ. It means one who is right. And no one could be right apart from God, given his character of omnipotence and omnipresence. When you are in Christ, know that you are standing not on your righteousness but the righteousness of Jesus Christ who died on the cross on your behalf for your sins. When you put on the breastplate of righteousness you must know that you are standing on the holiness of God who has redeemed you through the blood of his son on the cross having wiped out all the handwritings of requirements against you from the devil who had the power of death over you. Only Jesus Christ lived an obedient, perfect, and sinless life on earth to give us his righteousness in our standing with God. When God sees us, he sees the righteousness of his son through us, not our sins. We are completely justified by the righteousness of Christ. So, the devil has no right over you to kill you through disease, war, natural disasters, starvation, and plagues. It also means that the devil has no right over your children, job, finances, and your ministry. Practically it means that you may have committed sins in the past and the devil continues to remind you that you are not good enough to be a Christian. And your response to these accusations should be yes, I am not good enough to be a Christian and I do acknowledge that, but Christ died for me and I am standing on his righteousness for my salvation. You should know that you are elected by God and no one should bring charges against you as a Christian.

Having said that we must also be careful; even when we stand on the righteousness of Christ, we must not continue to walk in sins by sinning. What we must know is that walking in Christ does not mean that we are immune from sin. But God wants us not to sin wilfully. So, what he wants is that when we sin, we must be sincere by admitting and repenting of it never to repeat it. Walking in light does not mean sinless perfection but continuous repentance in agreement with God by confessing our sins to God and not hiding them from him as he already knows them anyway. The fact that he knows your sins before you even commit them shows that you cannot hide them from him. He just wants you to admit that he is aware of them because he is the master of your heart. So, you must be honest with him when you have sinned. It is also by doing so that the devil must not bring charges against you in the court of heaven, to block your blessings. To remind you God will do nothing until you have admitted your sins, that is when he can rebuke the devil. Covering up sins means that you are still in darkness and the light of God is not in you.

We are not able to produce our own righteousness because we are born into sin. In the garden of Eden, we know that our great grandfather sinned against God, and all of us are born into the sins of Adam. None of us is righteous before God that is why he had to send his son who came and died for us to regain our righteousness with him. Our attempt to produce or work our righteousness before him is disgusting to him. Even when we think that we have not committed any sin against God, our purest motives must glorify Jesus Christ as our saviour or else we will risk that our self-gratification becomes sinful and self-righteous. Anything humankind judges as good are abominable to God according to the prophet Isaiah. Because all of us have sinned and have fallen short of God's glory. We are never perfect on our own and we shall never be perfect on our own unless we put on Christ.

1 John 1:6-8: "If we confess our sins, he is faithful and righteous to forgive us our sins and to cleanse us from all unrighteousness". This verse indicates that God will only forgive you if you acknowledge your sins before him. He will only cleanse you of all unrighteousness if you admit that you have sinned against him and your fellow Christians. God hates sins and if you continue to hover over sins you will never succeed against the devil if you deny from God that you are a sinner. Confession of sins means that your success is guaranteed daily against the devil. You must have a blameless life in the presence of God when you admit and repent of your sins. The good news is that we cannot produce and work our righteousness as Christ has done it for us, but we must repent of those sins we commit daily. The entire mission of Christ on earth was to reconcile God's people back to him by the blood of his cross. The purpose of the cross was for him to nail all our requirements on himself for the sake of mercy, love, and kindness over us to give us salvation. All we need is to confess our sins daily and we will be right with God.

Being righteous does not only mean admitting your sins before God, but it also means that you must follow and do all the requirements the word of God demands from you. It also means following and respecting God's laws, statutes, commandments, and judgments. It means walking in his path and his ways. God wants us to pursue Christ's righteousness by imitating his character and conduct when he was here on earth. He wants us to turn away from our sinful nature and follow Christ's perfect ways. Our righteousness must begin in Christ and must be completed in Christ as God already perfected us through the righteousness of his son. We must be Christians who hear and do the word of God. If you hear the word and not do the word, then you are not a Christian at all. You are just no different from those outside the Christian faith. Listen to me very carefully; your success is not in what you hear but in what you do. "You must be a doer of the word not a hearer of the word." Righteousness means simply doing the right thing by God and people. Doing the right thing even when no one is watching but God is watching you. That is the righteousness God wants from you. Righteousness is the living acceptable standard needed from us by God. We must shun all sin and stay away from it if we are to be friends of God.

Chapter 9

The Shoes of Peace

St. Paul continues to expound on the whole Armour of God, in the book of Ephesians 6:15: "and your feet shod with the preparation of the gospel of peace." Here St. Paul compared the shoes worn by the Roman soldiers to the word of God preached by the servant of God to the people of the world. In short, he wants to emphasise to people who are the preachers to make the word of God as the shoes they must wear as they preach it to people. So, they must stand on the word as the source of peace but also as the ground on which they should stand. I hope this is very clear.

Let us go to the Roman soldiers' shoes and see why they were so important and so powerful. The Roman soldiers' shoes were not just normal shoes as they were made of bronze or brass that had greaves on the shoes themselves. The greaves started from the top of the knees all the way to the lower legs and rested on the upper portion of the feet. The whole design of these shoes was the basis from which modern army boots were designed and developed. The shoes themselves were made of two pieces of metal. The top and the bottom of the feet were covered with pieces of bronze or brass. The sides of the shoes were held together by many pieces of

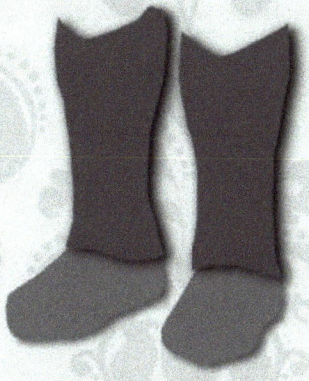

Source: https://www.christianbook.com

durable leather. On the bottom of these shoes, there were dangerous spikes that were two and a half centimetres long which were deadly in the battle or the combat situation. These shoes were not just normal shoes but dangerous shoes which were also weapons of war the Roman soldiers used to fight in a combat let alone to protect the foot.

In the same way, Roman soldiers were dependent on their shoes to fight the battle, St. Paul tells us that Christians must stand on the word of God as the basis on which they can preach to others. Just as Roman soldiers had confidence in their shoes, the preachers of the word of God must have confidence in the gospel of the Lord Jesus Christ not only as the source of our peace but also as a source of our knowledge, understanding and wisdom. Once you are equipped with the word of God in your life you are able to preach to others. It is from this position that you must fight the battle of faith against those who would challenge your knowledge about the word of God. Many people today do not believe the bible as the word of God let alone preaching to them. So, it is a fight to give the right information to them to win them to God's side. We must have the word of God which is the source of our peace to be grounded and stabilised in our lives, particularly in our minds and emotions. Peace is the foundation on which we stand and step out with confidence in faith believing that we cannot be moved by what we see happening around us and what we hear around us.

You can now appreciate why St. Paul called peace a "shoe" for a believer. Peace is the weapon Christians can use to withstand the darts and arrows of the devil. When we have peace of mind and peace of emotions, we are firmly secured, not to be brought down by the devil's schemes. No matter what the devil throws at us we will overcome it. When you have the peace of God in your life, you can walk through those dangerous thorny situations Satan plans on your way against your family, business, church, and job. If the devil can disturb your peace, then he can disturb your life. It is when we have peace of mind and emotions that we can think, speak, and act confidently on the subject matter of what we do. Grounded and stabilised by your peace guaranteed.

Peace of God is what will keep you safe amid storms of life in this world. What does the peace of God do in your life? It gives your confidence that you are not in charge of your own life and your own security but God. Satan may try to sabotage your peace by attacking your mind with dangerous thoughts and your emotions and dangerous situations around you, but all these can be in vain if you are grounded in the peace of God. Why is Satan doing this? Because Satan cannot just watch God's blessings pouring into your life without resistance, as he knows once you have money for example, sown into your life by God, you can go use it to win people back to God. Without a doubt, the peace of God is an awesome and powerful weapon to use against your enemy.

The great irony today is the fact that people of the world are yearning for peace and talking about peace, yet they do not know how to achieve peace because they have rejected the prince of peace our Lord Jesus Christ. Today you will see nations of the earth entering into agreements to maintain or to achieve peace among themselves and individuals looking for peace and achieving peace through jewellery, clothing, tattoos, cars, money, relationship, and power but all in vain. Because the world does not know how to get peace, but it also means that peace has different things attached to it to different people of the world. When nations or individuals seek God's peace, they are at rest even though everything else around them is wrong. Yes, it is a sincere wish for everyone to seek peace and to have peace, but it cannot be achieved without the author of peace, the Lord Jesus Christ. The only way people of the world can have peace is to have people who cannot just talk about peace but those who can work towards achieving peace who are also able to defend peace.

God's peace is totally different from world peace. World peace can only be achieved and maintained through the commitments and vows of the parties involved. This peace can just last so long as the parties are committed to it, but when one party violates its terms, it will be all over. World peace is expressed in food, drinks, songs, relationships, and entertainment. So, it is never a good peace and a permanent peace. God's peace can be permanent so long as he has his blessings upon it. God gives his peace without demand from anyone and for anything in return. The peace of God is given to us in the form of, joy, love, kindness, and righteousness. You can now see the differences between the peace of God and the peace of the world.

Peace Is Sown By Those Who Make Peace and Those Who Love Peace

Unless you have God in you and with you, you will never have genuine peace in your life, as it is him only who can supply true peace to you continuously and in abundance. You will have complete peace when you have a covenant with Jesus Christ the Prince of peace.

St. Paul referred to peace as "shoes of peace," in the book of Ephesians 6:10, denoting the importance shoes play in protecting the feet of the person from dangerous hazards in the conflict environment. The army officers, for example, wear boots for protection while on duty or during times of war. The workers in the manufacturing industry wear steel-capped boots to protect themselves from dangerous hazards during working hours. This means that the foot is an important part of the human body that needs proper protection.

In the same way, St. Paul referred to the saints or Christians who make peace among the people to be the peacemakers of the church. St. Paul treated these people as important members of the church as they rushed to make peace in conflict either in the church or elsewhere in the world. The gospel of Jesus Christ is the gospel of peace and so Jesus Christ himself is a prince of peace. We as Christians have the obligation to work for peace and live-in peace with ourselves.

The peace of the Lord which surpasses human understanding does not necessarily mean not having problems but rather facing them with complete calm and coolness of mind. It means not worrying too much about the problems as our God is in full control. The peace of God is not given in exchange for something unlike the peace of the world where both parties to peace demands offer in return, to achieve peace. The peace of God is not unconditional unlike the peace of the world where parties demand conditions to be met by their other party to peace.

When you received the Lord Jesus Christ as your saviour know that you have received the prince of peace. It is through his flesh and blood that he was able to reconcile us back to God as a propitiation of our sins. By his death on the cross, he was able to make his peace rule in our hearts. It is freely given to those who believe in Christ.

The only way Christians can overcome the devil schemes is to let the peace of Christ dominate their thoughts, speech, and actions in their relationship with the other believers and non-believers in the world. Where there are conflicts and misunderstandings, we must be there as peacemakers not as fighters. Matthew 5:9 says, "Blessed are the peacemakers, for they shall be called sons of God." You can also be called a son of God when you are a peacemaker. Peacemakers in the church are in the ministry of reconciliation according to St. Paul. We must be diligent as Christians in holding on to the unity of the church of God through the bond of peace. Peace is the glue that keeps the Christians together in times of troubles or persecutions. May the peace of the living God dwell and work richly in you to be a good peacemaker in the church of God and in the world as well. If you are a Christian going through tribulation, persecution, sickness, distress, famine, peril, or war, know that Jesus Christ has crushed Satan under his feet giving millions of Christians freedom to have peace within themselves and with God. Matthew 11:28-30 says, "Come to Me, all you who labour and are heavy laden, and I will give you rest. Take My yoke upon you and learn from Me, for I am gentle and lowly in heart, and you will find rest for your souls. For My yoke is easy and My burden is light."

Christians must always be representatives of Christ in making peace among themselves and in the world. The gospel of Jesus Christ is the gospel of peace; that is why it cannot be imposed on those who reject it, such as Islam and other religions of the world which are maintained and spread through violence. May the person who will read this be turned into a peacemaker in Jesus Christ's name. Peace-Peace-Peace.

Power of information: You cannot have and experience true peace on earth until you have the owner and the master of peace- Jesus Christ. This is for those who are going through tough times right now: hold your peace (rest on his peace); remain at rest (stand your ground – you do not need to fight the battle – He is doing that); Keep doing what you are doing (pray, fast, praise, and read the bible), and Let God fight the battle for you, for he is the battle. He is the master of all things. "All things work together for good to those who love God, to those who are called according to his purpose." *(Romans 8:28).*

Chapter 10

The Helmet of Salvation

The most important part of the human body that not only Romans protect, but everyone around the world protects with other devices including the helmet, is our head. Even God himself gave the head a special consideration by creating a special protection device called the skull to protect our mind and our brain from external injuries. The purpose of the helmet in the ideal world setting is to protect our minds from injury during the war, work situations, construction, sports, motorcycles, and heavy vehicles. The reason why the brain is protected heavily is that if it is damaged everything about us is damaged. In other words, there can never be a fully functioning human being when there is damage to the brain.

The Roman emperor knew this, that a good soldier is the one that is highly protected including his brain protection. And so, they had to design a helmet that not only protects the head but also the shoulders and the neck of the soldiers. The Roman soldiers' helmets were not just simple designed pieces of metal to put on the head, they were beautiful and fascinating pieces of weaponry metal that were very intricate and ornate. They were designed in a way that had a piece to protect the jaws and cheeks from damage by their enemy weaponry. The lining in the inner

FIGHTING THE INVISIBLE ENEMY

The Helmet of Salvation

Take the helmet of salvation
—Ephesians 6:17

The Roman soldier's helmet was fashioned from bronze or iron. Two hinged cheek-pieces protected the sides of the soldier's face. For the sake of comfort, soldiers frequently lined their helmets with sponge or felt. At the time of Christ, a crest with a plume of horse's hair was placed on top of Roman helmets.

The Roman soldier's helmet protected his skull and neck from his enemy's weapons and falling debris. By AD 60, the centurions' plumes were dyed various colors to allow soldiers to distinguish quickly between the rank of different officers.[5]

The helmet of salvation points to God's ultimate victory over the forces of evil. Jesus' death on the cross and his resurrection from the dead provides all believers with freedom from the bondage of sin, and with eternal life with God in heaven.

To put on "the helmet of salvation" is to—
- Have assurance that Jesus has saved you, not because of good deeds, but because of his mercy. 2 Timothy 1:9
- Know that every believer is a "new creation," no longer living for selfish purposes but living for the Lord. 2 Corinthians 5:17
- Accept that you are in a battle and will be persecuted for believing in Christ. Keep the faith and you will be blessed. Matthew 5:11, 12
- Look forward to being delivered into eternal life. John 3:16
- Know that God will forgive his followers when they fall and ask for forgiveness. 1 John 1:9

[The LORD] put on righteousness as his breastplate, and the helmet of salvation on his head
—Isaiah 59:17
You also were included in Christ when you heard the word of truth, the gospel of your salvation. Having believed, you were marked in him with a seal, the promised Holy Spirit. —Eph. 1:13
But since we belong to the day, let us be self-controlled, putting on faith and love as a breastplate, and the hope of salvation as a helmet — 1 Thessalonians 5:8

gallic—helmet
centurion—Roman military officer who commanded approximately 100 soldiers.

Source: https://www.christianbook.com

part had spongy materials that made them soft and comfortable to be worn by the soldiers. In short, they were not just the weapons of war but also weapons of beauty the soldiers were proud to wear. What made the Roman soldiers confident in their service for their nation, was partly these helmets that distinguished them among the armies of the nations.

St. Paul compared our salvation to these helmets worn by Roman soldiers on their head to protect their important organ, the brain. It is the only thing we have from God for our lives. Salvation is the only priceless thing we will have from God if we are to stay firm in his work of salvation. Just as heads had special consideration by the Roman emperor to be well protected in the Roman battle against their enemies, it is also true that our minds are the target by Satan to immobilise us from the work of God's kingdom. As Christians, we must take our work of salvation very seriously. The devil will bombard our minds with different thoughts and information for us to disregard the importance of salvation. But we must put on a helmet against all those thoughts as our end time goal, which is our salvation in our Lord Jesus Christ. If you cannot wear your salvation in your mind like a helmet, then evil will come and chopped off the benefits of your salvation away from you and your belief system. Very important indeed that your salvation through Jesus Christ is what has brought you peace with God. I wish everybody would understand this, that there is nothing we can pay to go and live with God in Heaven. Facing the devil without the idea of your salvation in your mind will be a blow to you. No matter what the devil throws in your way, know that you are already predestined for heaven. And there is nothing you and I could be prouder about than this work of the cross by our Lord Jesus Christ.

Satan will attempt to destroy your salvation by destroying your mind and your belief system through diseases such as Alzheimer, stress, depression, paranoia, and all forms of mental disorders so that you cannot concentrate on the things of God. When this happens then he is the winner. You cannot imagine what you can do to the devil when you have a healthy mind. Once our minds do not function in the way they were created by God, then our emotions and our will are impeded from carrying out their activities in the right way and right order. But all these are defeated when you know that Jesus Christ's victory on the cross and his resurrection from death was for you and me to go and live with him in heaven. We are a new creation in Christ not because of our work but because of his victory against sin on the cross for us all (the Christians). This is a fact we should be proud of and we must not let the devil intimidate us from this fact.

If there is one thing and one thing only you will need God for, then it is the salvation of your soul as there is nothing you can give to God in exchange for it, not to rot in hell. Salvation is the act of a person, group, community, society, and nations being saved or delivered from sins, transgression, and iniquity against God. Sin is a rebellion against God which is punishable by death or for which the penalty is living away from God. We know that sin entered the world through Adam and was removed from the world through one man, our Lord Jesus Christ. When Adam and Eve sinned, the whole world was cursed by God; the land was cursed, the man (Adam) was cursed and Satan who deceived them was also cursed. As a result of Adam's rebellion, humankind was isolated from God. Humans were dead in their own trespasses, living on earth and going to hell afterlife.

To correct this, God out of His mercy and his kindness had to send his own son into the world to lay down his own life on the cross on behalf of humanity to save us from death. Even as Christ has done this, people who continue to commit their own individual sins can still go to hell because of their unbelief and they must also know that God has zero-tolerance of sin and no mercy for those who reject his son as a saviour and as a result, nothing will save them from going to hell. People who have lived this life and die without believing Jesus Christ, will go to hell. It is through Jesus Christ that we obtain the mercy and grace of God, for our salvation. There is no other name in heaven above, on earth and underneath earth by which people can be saved, than the name of our Lord Jesus Christ. To this effect, we must take our lives here on earth and what we do with them as a serious business, as choices we make in life with or without God will determine our fate when we die. As I always say, once you are dead, it is no longer you who decides where you will go-whether it is heaven or hell- but God. When you accept the Lord Jesus Christ as your personal saviour then you have chosen your afterlife, and when you reject the Lord Jesus Christ then you have chosen external condemnation (hell). The following verses of the bible tell us very clearly and explicitly:

"Nor is there salvation in any other, for there is no other name under heaven given among men by which we must be saved" (Acts 4:12).

"For there is one God and one Mediator between God and men, the Man Christ Jesus, who gave Himself a ransom for all ..." (1 Timothy 2:5).

"There is one body and one Spirit ... one Lord, one faith, one baptism, one God and Father of all, who is above all, and through all, and in you all" (Ephesians 4:4).

Jesus said to him, "I am the way, the truth, and the life. No one comes to the Father except through Me" (John 14:6).

"I am the door. If anyone enters by Me, he will be saved, and will go in and find pasture ... I have come that they may have life and that they may have it more abundantly" (John 10:9).

Jesus said to her, "I am the resurrection and the life, he who believes in Me, though he may die, he shall live. And whoever lives and believes in Me shall never die" (John 11:25).

Then Jesus spoke to them again, saying, "I am the light of the world. He who follows Me shall not walk in darkness, but have the light of life" (John 8:12).

And Jesus said to them, "I am the bread of life. He who comes to Me shall never hunger and he who believes in Me shall never thirst" (John 6:35).

"I am the living bread which came down from heaven. If anyone eats of this bread, he will live forever; and the bread that I shall give is My flesh, which I shall give for the life of the world" (John 6:51).

"Whoever believes in Him should not perish but have eternal life. For God so loved the world that He gave His only begotten Son, that whoever believes in Him should not perish but have everlasting life" (John 3:15-16).

"He who believes in the Son has everlasting life; and he who does not believe the Son shall not see life, but the wrath of God abides on him" (John 3:36).

"Therefore I said to you that you will die in your sins; for if you do not believe that I am He, you will die in your sins" (John 8:24).

"Most assuredly, I say to you, he who hears My word and believes in Him who sent Me has everlasting life, and shall not come into judgment, but has passed from death to life" (John 5:24).

"And this is the testimony: that God has given us eternal life and this life is in His Son. He who has the Son has life; He who does not have the Son of God does not have life" (1 John 5:11).

"And we have seen and testify that the Father has sent the Son as Saviour of the world. Whoever confesses that Jesus is the Son of God, God abides in him, and he in God" (1 John 4:14).

I do not know about you but there is nothing I am grateful to God almighty more than the salvation of my soul. If it were not because of God's mercy and kindness nothing you and I would have used to get it, not even gold, silver, bronze, power, and money. It is an exciting opportunity to be able to go and live in heaven with the father of creation where there will be no more sickness, natural disasters, poverty, starvation, hunger, hatred, jealousy, wars, and death. All these scary things in the world will be no more. Think about that. Salvation, while we live here on earth, protects and delivers us from the power of sin once we accept our Lord Jesus Christ as our personal saviour. What the devil does not want you to know is that you have salvation secured for you by our Lord Jesus Christ when he went to the cross on your behalf for your soul to be saved, and hence Satan has no power to take away from you. Once you know this, then Satan has no more power to control, manipulate and kill you. With this mind no matter what the devil throws at you it will never prosper – whether it is sickness, poverty, hatred, disasters, or family crisis. None of these will have a stronghold on you. This is the true hope we have in God that will keep us going here on earth no matter how difficult things get sometimes in our lives.

Blessed be the God and Father of our Lord Jesus Christ, who according to His abundant mercy has begotten us again to a living hope through the resurrection of Jesus Christ from the dead, to an inheritance incorruptible and undefiled and that does not fade away, reserved in heaven for you, who are kept by the power of God through faith for a salvation ready to be revealed in the last time. In this, you greatly rejoice, though now for a little while, if need be, you have been grieved by various trials, that the genuineness of your faith, being much more precious than gold that perishes, though it is tested by fire, may be found to praise, honour, and glory at the revelation of Jesus Christ, whom having not seen you love. Though now you do not see Him, yet believing, you rejoice with joy inexpressible and full of glory, receiving the end of your faith—the salvation of your souls. (1 Peter 1:3-9)

It is absolutely the will of God that every single soul is saved, yet the choice still rests with you whether you can accept his kindness and mercy or reject it. So, God has left the entire matter in your hands to make your own decision to believe in his only begotten son Jesus Christ to go and live with him in heaven after this life or you can reject him voluntarily and go and live in hell away from God. The decision is now yours to decide. God will never force himself on anyone who rejects his salvation through his son Jesus Christ.

"God our Saviour, who desires ALL MEN to be saved and to come to the knowledge of the truth" (1 Timothy 2:4).

"The Lord is not slack concerning His promise, as some count slackness, but is longsuffering toward us, not willing that any should perish but that all should come to repentance" (2 Peter 3:9).

"For there is no distinction between Jew and Greek, for the same Lord over all is rich to all who call upon Him. For WHOEVER calls upon the name of the Lord shall be saved" (Romans 10:12).

Lest any man should boast, we are saved by the grace of God through faith. There is nothing we have done or could do to get salvation. Because of God's mercy in our lives, we are redeemed from the hands of the Devil. While we were all sinners Christ died for us. This means that before we even became a Christian God had given his own son's life on the cross for us who would later believe in the name of his son Jesus Christ. So, none is righteous to deserve the salvation of God. So, our faith in God qualifies us for the grace, which in turn gives us salvation.

"For by grace you have been saved through faith, and that not of yourselves; it is the gift of God, not of works, lest anyone should boast" (Ephesians 2:8).

"Knowing that a man is not justified by the works of the law but by faith in Jesus Christ for by the works of the law no flesh shall be justified" (Galatians 2:16).

"Therefore, by the deeds of the law no flesh will be justified in His sight, for by the law is the knowledge of sin for all have sinned and fall short of the glory of God" (Romans 3:20,23).

Through salvation, we have the righteousness of Christ. So, we have the peace of God through the works of Jesus Christ on the cross. He died for us to have peace with God, correcting our rebellion against himself through the first human, Adam. When Adam sinned in the garden of Eden against God the communication between humankind and God was severed, which was later restored by Jesus Christ, making peace between humanity and God. That is why God does not want any single soul in hell because it has cost his son's life to save us from the death of our sins. No matter what you think your sins are, God will never reject you based on that because his son has already done it on the cross for you. All you need is just to believe in him, and you will be saved. When we continue to commit sins when we are saved, we must immediately repent (but it must be unintentional). God will always forgive us when we wholeheartedly confess our sins before him and with complete repentance from our sin, never to repeat them again. This is not to say that we must sin wilfully, for God to continue to forgive us. When you commit sin with your full knowledge before committing it, then you are testing God and there will be a penalty or punishment for it. Never test God. It is the sins that we commit unknowingly that God can forgive us for, not those that we commit with our full knowledge.

"For He made Him who knew no sin to be sin for us, that we might become the righteousness of God in Him" (2 Corinthians 5:21).

"But God demonstrates His own love toward us, in that while we were still sinners, Christ died for us. Much more then, having now been justified by His blood, we shall be saved from wrath through Him" (Romans 5:8).

"Repent therefore and be converted, that your sins may be blotted out, so that times of refreshing may come from the presence of the Lord" (Acts 3:19).

"If we confess our sins, He is faithful and just to forgive us our sins and to cleanse us from all unrighteousness" (1 John 1:9).

"If you confess with your mouth the Lord Jesus and believe in your heart that God has raised Him from the dead, you will be saved. For with the heart one believes to righteousness, and with the mouth confession is made to salvation" (Romans 10:9).

Although the salvation of our souls is the result of our faith in God when we leave this earth, that does not mean that it should be the only centre and focus of our work and attention. Many Christians believe in the salvation of their souls but also need to live this life now with the full force of heaven operating within them and from them, to carry out our God-given assignment here on earth. While on earth we must operate with full heaven requirements for us on earth. This is the true idea of being the salts of the earth as Christians. Satan was defeated on the cross for us to live this life on earth with full authority and power. Adam and Eve lost to Satan, and authority was restored to us by Christ to dominate the earth and subdue it without interference by Satan. Let him not lie to you, he is a defeated useless liar. Yes, indeed a great chunk of this earth still lies under his authority, but nonetheless, he has no control over Christians under the kingdom of God.

We are God's ambassadors on earth, with a heaven specific assignment, which is our life purpose. We do not have to think of rushing to heaven while we have not fulfilled our assignment here on earth, for which we were sent here. The major area among which we must have a sphere of influence while here on earth is politics, to see that there is a maintenance of a peaceful human society. Not only politics, but every area of human society demands that Christians be involved in some degree of influence, not Christian activism against the government and over human social issues. Whether it is the right to vote, holding political office, praying for leaders, and paying taxes to the government, or preaching the word of God to politicians, Christians should be attentive to how the government is run and how human society is ruled. Or else we will fail the assignment of being the salt of the earth. Somebody may ask why I single out politics? Because it is where major policies and laws affecting Christians are made. This area plus other areas such as community organisations and business organisations necessitate voices to be heard as Christians. We must bring to life our Christian values of love, peace, unity, and harmony to many areas of human society such as family, education, medicine, and the environment. We must make sure that these areas are dominated by Christians to bring the culture of heaven to earth. We must know that we are the only apparatus for the change God can use to influence earth with the heaven culture. Hence, we must make ourselves available as vessels of God to use for dominion and rulership of the earth in whatever areas God has called us to rule in.

While carrying out our God-given assignment on earth, we must daily be seeking the counsel and guidance of the Holy Spirit as the Godhead's representative here on earth. I must emphasise this very clearly because without the help of the Holy Spirit it will be impossible to carry out our assignments. The only way we can become children of God is to have the Holy Spirit working and operating through us. As Christians we must know that the true temple of the Holy Spirit is not churches, we go to pray to God, but our bodies. It is only through the spirit of God that we can achieve much in this life including our God given assignments. The gifts of the Holy Spirit such as healing, faith, miracles, knowledge, wisdom, understanding, administration, and fruits of the Holy Spirit such as love, joy, peace, kindness, long-suffering, and many more must become available to us when we make our bodies the temple of the Holy Spirit in order to carry out and to fulfil our God-given assignments here on earth.

Chapter 11

The Sword of Spirit

There is no important armour like the word of God to the believer. You can have all the protective equipment but if you have nothing at your hands to fight your enemy then you will be defeated in a battle. St. Paul compared the word of God to the swords used by the Roman soldiers in the battle. Guess what? St. Paul even said that the word of God is more powerful than the physical swords of the Roman soldiers they relied on to fight the battle. If the Roman soldiers were confident in their swords to defeat their enemies, what about us who have the word of God in our hands as the weapon for our warfare against our enemies? The victory is ours and will always be ours so long as we are in the word and holding the word in our hands.

The Roman soldiers had two swords namely spatha and gladius. The spatha was a little longer than gladius but they were both used for battle but in different situations, depending on the enemy attack. Gladius was in most cases the deadly sword used by the Roman soldier against his enemy because of its length and it was the one St. Paul was referring to in Ephesians 6:17. The gladius was like a dagger used close to the face, close-up, hand to hand combat, and always one to one op-

Source: http://www.theyouareproject.com

ponent. Gladius could not be seen by the enemy sometimes in close combat, which made it deadly to the enemy. The blades were double-edged and needle-sharp at all points allowing great damage to the opponent's heart or midsection. It was, without doubt, a deadly weapon that could kill quickly within a short period of time.

The word of God is the spiritual sword used by the Christians against their enemy. The only thing you can defeat the devil with is the bible. There is no book on earth that talks about the spiritual world more than the bible. There is no book on earth that talks about the past, present, and future of the world we live in more than the Bible. The Bible is not just a history book but a source of life for those who apply it in their own lives. What God says he must do in his word, he does. There is no condition of human beings that the bible has not addressed. The bible is the open book exam for your life.

If God used his word to bring to existence the entire universe including the heavens, then how can you just hold it in your hands as a helpless object? I want you to know today that you are carrying a deadly weapon in your hands, which you could use against sickness, natural disasters, financial difficulty, family breakdown and even the future generations of your family. It is a sword against depression, stress, and suicidal thoughts. There is a war, and you must use your sword to fight it. Going to church every day and hearing the good sermons on Sundays does not change your situation. What changes your situation is when you begin to apply what you have learned in your situation. I cannot emphasise this enough. The bible warns us not to be hearers of the word but doers of the word.

Listen; "Your spirit (your communication antenna with God) and your soul (will, intellect and emotions) are dependent upon the word of God." Once you have disconnected them from the daily bread (Word of the Bible), you are a dead person walking, subject to the attack of the devil at any time. The spirit and soul have nothing to do with your natural food. They are of God and they need the word of God to survive just as your body needs food and drink to survive. If both are without the word of God, then are just a malnourished soul and spirit. They will go back to God, but only when you believe in the message of salvation. Your natural food is there to support the tent (body), which is the incubator of your spirit and soul. When the devil attacks your body and not your spirit and your soul, you will never die. I hope I have made that clear. That is why Jesus defeated the devil because he was using his own words from the father. Scary and complicated as it may be, but there is no word without Jesus and there is no Jesus with the word. They are one. That is why when he was here on earth, he never said anything wrong about the scriptures. But he said there was something wrong with religion. He was critical of the Pharisees, Scribes and Sadducees as impediments to the God Kingdom. Today people are killing themselves in the name of God through religion. Today innocent people are being abused in churches in the name of God.

The Bible, according to the scriptures above, is resounding yes, a word of God written by those people inspired by God. It is not a book written by religious scholars for their interests. It is important to note that God is not religion and religion is not God. This is a very big wild claim that may be a subject for discussion soon. In short, the bible is for God and religion is for people. There are two distinctive things altogether. The Bible was written by God's prophets using God's instructions and revelations. ***Amos 3:7*** says, "Surely the Lord God does nothing unless He reveals His secret to His servants the prophets. It is for the good of humanity that he gets his word to be written down*". **Hosea 4:6*** says, "My people are destroyed for lack of knowledge. Because you have rejected knowledge, I also will reject you from being a priest for Me; Because you have forgotten the law of your God, I also will forget your children." Your mission here on earth is for God not for you (think about the book of life after death). Where you will be asked –What did you do for God while you were on earth? If the Bible is the word of God, then why can't we believe it, yet its scriptures are life to those who find them? Why is it so difficult to believe God's Word? Here are the answers: the main strategy of the devil is to get you to doubt the word of God and for you to become a prime target for destruction; Once he gets you to doubt the existence of God, his son, and his spirit, then you are set for hell; The devil is up to no good, as he is already judged by God and set for hell. His strategy is to take you to hell, so you are dead forever. Think about that.

Let us look at the human being as a tripartite being (spirit, soul, and body), and the importance of the word of God to a human being. Think about this: the human being's innermost part is spirit and soul, which should be dependent upon the word of God, as their daily bread (Bible Scriptures). This means you must read the word of God every day to feed your spirit and soul (will, intellect and emotions). Another great important aspect of the Bible revealed. This has nothing to do with our natural food (dairy, cereals, fruits, and vegetables). This is the only part that communicates with the Kingdom of God and particularly the Holy Spirit (residence). So, when you quote the word of God in the scriptures during prayer, it will warrant a response from God, because you are talking to him. ***Exodus 34:28*** says, "So he was there with the Lord forty days and forty nights; he neither ate bread nor drank water. And He wrote on the tablets the words of the covenant, the Ten Commandments." So, Moses' inner being (spirit and soul) became powerful in the presence of God, as his physical body became weak. What it means here in our daily situations, is that now you have power which you can use to decree and declare words in the areas of your condition where you are attacked by the devil and be healed. These could be in the areas of family problems, healthy, education, business, and natural disasters. We tend to focus a lot on feeding our physical bodies which are of no use to God at all. Our natural food is there to support our internal being working to perform well. If you want to connect to God, then you must focus on your spirit and soul. ***Colossians 3:16*** says**,** "Let the word of Christ dwell in you richly in all wisdom, teaching and admonishing one another in psalms and hymns and spiritual songs, singing with grace in your hearts to the Lord."

Words are important to us. The power of life and death is in the words we speak (David versus Goliath). The power of our success or failure is in the words we speak and believe about ourselves (Prophet Elijah called fire from heaven). Words also determined the outcomes of the wars we fought (Ronald Reagan in the hostage crisis of 1979), with the Iranian government. The words we put on paper (books) come because of our imaginations, thoughts, and creativity in our minds (soul), which becomes ideas to later shape our vision and mission in life. It is these ideas that become important human facts, principles, and theories governing our way of life in the communities, societies, cultures, traditions, religions, government, and other institutions of the world. It is these human words that also give individuals a distinctive status in the institutions of learning, that we are proud of. But this is all based on human wisdom which has nothing at all to do with God. People today go to universities to study other people's theories and principles, and later claim to be educated. This, in fact, shows that our knowledge is just as good as the knowledge of the owners of theories. People passionately believe in other people's knowledge (human scholars) in measuring their success as human beings. If our success can be determined by other people's words (Ideas), then why can't we also apply the same to God's words?

Also, as human beings, we believe in the science community report which is based on carbon dating that is a total lie. Carbon dating is based on carbon remains that have wasted away over the years to determine the number of years of humans, plants, and animals, which once lived on earth. Carbon dating has one purpose: a chemical analysis used to determine the age of organic materials based on their content of the radioisotope carbon-14 believed to be reliable up to 40,000 years. Hence, it is important to note that the Science community believes in the discovery of things but not the creation of things. So, who created everything which we are so dependent upon today in the world? Additionally, all medication is dependent upon God's plants and animals. So, where is human invention outside God's creation? Interesting indeed!!!!

Human beings also believe in the report of the medical institutions (doctors), who treat the symptoms of the diseases they cannot even see. For example, once the doctors pronounced the symptoms of rarely curable diseases such as cancer, Ebola and HIV Aids, their spirit crashed within them immediately. People become so desperate in their attempt to save their lives by accepting any treatment given to them following the doctor's instructions, without questioning side effects. They just believed. So, the spirit within them gives up without resistance to the message of death pronounced upon them. Mostly what killed people is not the disease itself, but the succumbing of the spirit within humans, as it has no other source of hope at all. Sometimes they may be lucky to be given medications for life. They take them without rejection. This is another human belief from another human report. Human wisdom can be so fatal without God. If humans can believe everything which is not of God, then why can the same concept apply to God's word? Humans should begin to reject another human's report and turn to their creator (God), and they will surely live. Begin to quote God's scriptures on healing and you will be instantly healed. That is the good news to those who have been totally failed by the medical systems and government systems. With God, there is a future for those whose lives hang in the balance between life and death.

"Every mountain the devil places in your way is not there to kill you, but rather to reveal God in you." The greater the condition or the situation you are in, the greater is the call of God in your life. God entices people using worse situations or conditions to work with you eventually. Greatest information revealed. God in the beginning created you and predestined you. This means that every difficult thing the devil placed on your way back to God, is a shadow of death, as King David said. But it can be a real death, which can take you to hell if you do not turn to God for help.

Believe in the word and you will never fail. This is a hundred per cent assurance from me. God can do nothing for you unless you pray. Prayer is communication with God. But you must quote the word to suit your situation. My job is to bring God's revelation as close to you as I humanly can.

Undoubtedly, the bible is a source of wisdom for those who read it with understanding. It is only God who will open the mind of your understanding for the bible to make sense to you and for you to ultimately have the understanding of it. The bible is the word of God and you are a child of God, and when you bring these two together, it will form a powerful bond that will enable you to triumph over every situation you are in. God guaranteed that his word will never return to him void in any situation it was sent forth for. The in-depth knowledge about God's word gives you power over the demons. The Bible is the source of verses that address issues of each condition you are in- whether it is sickness, poverty, divorce, vision, and mission. The bible says you shall decree and declare a word over your situation, and you will be set free.

Besides, the bible is a source of hope and joy. A lot of people try to have peace in the material possessions of this world, yet they cannot, because they were not meant to be at peace that way. Even when you have garnered a considerable amount of money, power, and many other possessions one will still lack peace, joy, and hope because in all these things there is no true happiness of the real you (which is the spirit man). While you feed the body with the material, things, your spirit, and soul still miss out on these things. The food for soul and spirit is the word of God. Every time you feel you are down you can go into the bible and find scriptures that will bring hope, joy and peace to your spirit and soul. St. Paul said, "For the kingdom of God is not about eating and drinking, but righteousness, peace, and joy in the Holy Spirit". *(Romans 14:17).* So, what you need is to study the word, believe the word and keep it in your heart. This will bring joy to the inner of you.

More importantly, the word of God is the light to our path in this life on earth. What God has given to every single person on the planet no matter what amount of material riches they have, is the future that we do not know. We are not sure what will happen to us in the next few minutes, hours, days, weeks, months, and years ahead of us, but it is all in the bible. It is only the bible that can tell you what will happen to you in the future through the guidance of the holy spirit. By reading and studying the Bible you will learn and gain knowledge, wisdom and understanding of the future. Without the Bible, you have no future in this world.

Chapter 12

Breaking the Demonic Strongholds in Your Life and your Family

Your Strategy for the Battle

What all Christians must know is this; even though there is still a real war raging against us on this earth by Satan, it has already been won by our Lord Jesus Christ on the cross on our behalves. ***But God demonstrates His own love toward us, in that while we were still sinners, Christ died for us (Romans 5:8). NKJV.*** You might be confused, why is this? Well, God defeated Satan on cross and allowed him to run the world under those who rejected God. Satan also continues to tempt the Christians, who still live sinful lives but with limited power over them to commit to their work of salvation, if they quickly realised, they are under temptation return to God. Put it in a better context, God is a holy God, and he does not want anyone to come to heaven with fleshly sins even though they are Christians. You must first die to sins before you will have your salvation and be destined for heaven. You will agree with me that there are still Christians, even though they are saved, who continue to commit sins in defiance and against their Christians values and beliefs with no repentance and sometimes in denial, yet God is watching them. That is why Satan continues to tempt those Christians who live alive of sin, so that they can repent fully in order not to lose their salvation. For example, have you questioned yourself why, in the churches today, you will still witness, sexual immorality, violence, homosexuality, jealousy, hatred, false preaching, deceptions, thuggery, drunkenness, idolatry and so on and so forth?

What separated humanity from God was the issue of sin which is still prevalent today in our societies. Humankind is wicked in nature; even if God had to remove the devil, people would still reject God. The most dangerous thing God has ever given humanity is the "human will," the ability to do what we want without interferences by others or even God for that matter. What gets us to sin are the choices we make within our **"wills,"** for our lives whether good or bad. It is within our own "will," that we do not want God to tell us that it is bad to steal, covet, hate, envy, fight, gossip, slander, and offense. What got Adam and Eve into trouble with God, was the choice they made by themselves to speak to the devil even though God had warned them not to. Without a shadow of a doubt, you are now convinced just as I am convinced as to why God allowed the devil back into the Christians lives even though they believed in him. So, it is for your good that he allowed Satan to tempt you, that you may come out perfect for heaven. In nutshell, you have a choice within your **"will,"** to grant permission to either God or Satan into your life. You can bring hell or heaven upon your life. The choice is yours to live your life holy or unholy.

When God created Adam and Eve, he created two clean people and their clean genealogy to follow. God created humankind as a good friend to have a good daily conversation (together) in his presence (Garden of Eden), about how the affairs of earth could be run by humankind that he created in his own image. With this in mind, this question could be asked; What happened to this good intention of God over humankind? Why is there so much destruction and human suffering today in the world? These questions plus many others you could ask are functional to your very existence on earth and your survival in it.

God created a perfect human being with good intention but Adam and Eve and the rest of their genealogy following were tempted to reject God for Satan –

the angel of God who rebelled against him early on in heaven. One could ask this question; How did this happen? Well, Adam and Eve disobeyed God's instruction not to listen to the other voices in the Garden of Eden. They were told not to eat from the tree of knowledge of good and evil. So, by their own will, they chose to bring disaster upon themselves and their genealogy following by rebelling against God's instruction. Through this ordeal, the disaster came to humanity that would later be the cause of the human beings suffering on earth. God out of anger had to cursed humanity, the land (which is the earth we are in), and Satan who deceived them, with eternal condemnation in hell.

Humanity was created immediately after the Satan rebellion in heaven to replace Satan over the running of God property (earth). Certainly, something did happen that was unique in a way, and this was the creation of humanity in God's image and likeness. The bible is very clear that no angels were created in God's image including Satan. This action of God makes Satan jealous against mankind, and since then he had to wage war against mankind, who called on the name of God and who takes care of His creation. So, there is a war against you and your family because of this action of God.

This question could be asked; How does this war play out in your life and that of your family? Once you become a Christian, whether you know it or not, the devil is at war with you and your family. Your action indicates to him that you have denounced him and his kingdom for God, who is his enemy. God is an enemy of Satan because he has created you in His own image. So, the answer goes back to you being the centre of the battle. The battle plays out this way in your life: the devil's ultimate goal is to deny you access to God, who is your creator and who also has a real purpose for your life. He does it this way; for those who believe in God (Christians), Satan fights them through diseases, family separation and madness and those who don't believe in God, he fights them by making sure that they doubt the existence of God, Jesus Christ and the Holy Spirit. So he keeps the unbelievers away from God in the darkness of their senses and beliefs through wars to reject God.

When the war or the battle rages against you and your family, he makes sure that it is heated up in order for you to reject God and his cross, redemption, salvation and more importantly your purpose here on Earth. He has to make sure that your identity in God is taken away together with your God given blessings here on earth. Have you wondered now about when you were growing up, you had big dreams of being one day a president, prime minister, manager, doctor, lawyer, businessperson, anthropologist, family person, and so forth? But have you noticed something? These big dreams are without God!!! Why is this? Because he knows you cannot achieve them without God. Please do not get me wrong; these big dreams are God-given but what Satan does is to attack the processes of achieving them in life. By the time you attempt to get them achieved without God, Satan will frustrate your ways or even kill you prematurely before you achieve them. Satan has to make sure that you are not connected to God as much as possible by destroying your identity. Why is this? Because if you connect to God you will achieve all your dreams as he is your true creator and the true giver of your dreams. Listen to me carefully; your big dreams are God-given, and you cannot achieve them without God. When God created you, He created you with your assignment intact in you. For those who **come** across this book, can I tell you this; the kingdom of God is within you together with your God-given assignment. This is proven by these beautiful words of God to prophet ***Jeremiah 1:5; "Before I formed you in the womb I knew you; Before you were born I sanctified you; I ordained you a prophet to the nations."***

The devil and his demons are after your God-given assignment and the entirety of God's orders for creation to distort it, if not to destroy it altogether. He does this in several ways including but not limited to the following**:** marriages and families, jobs, health, finances, relationships.

What to Do if Satan Attacks Your Family and Marriage

One thing the devil hates the most is the family and marriages done in God's order of creation. The order of God's creation is that the man was created first and he is the head of the family, and later woman and children who are under the custodianship of man. Let me be clear, the man represents God in the unit (family). Watch this, "woman was created for man and not man for Woman**. *(Genesis 2:18).*** When God created Adam, he gave him the responsibility to protect, provide and to take care of the entire universe around him including the extended families of God. For example, that is why you will see great men, besides taking care of their families, also have the responsibility to take care of God's creation. Scientists look after the natural environment including animals and plants; presidents look after people of the nations, and doctors look after the sick people. This is not to say that there are no great women who are experts in these fields, but the primary responsibility of a woman was to take care of the family, particularly the children. The biggest role God has ever given a woman when she was created was to be the company for her husband and to give birth to children who will be the next generations of the inhabitants of the earth. This to me is the greatest responsibility God has ever given women. In nutshell, although they seem (men and women) to have different roles, the roles are intertwined. The man needs the service of a woman and the woman needs the service of a man. So, there cannot be a man without a woman, there cannot be a woman without a man. Isn't this work of God marvellous? What God created works in perfect order, and it is always beautiful. But what is important in all of this as a family, is to be united to achieve much in this life, and to call for God's protection in unison, for the family to remain united in the longevity God has given you on earth. The husbands must love their wives and wives must also love their husbands and children must love both their parents. Love in the family is the bond of perfection. In order for you to overcome the schemes of the devil as a family, you must remain in love. This is the greatest verse in the bible I can give you because it has kept me going as well in difficult moments in my relationship. Look at these beautiful verses of the bible: ***1 Corinthians 13:5-8 "Love suffers long and is kind; love does not envy; love does not parade itself, is not puffed up; does not behave rudely, does not seek its own, is not provoked, thinks no evil; does not rejoice in iniquity, but rejoices in the truth; bears all things, believes all things, hopes all things, endures all things. Love never fails. But whether there are prophecies, they will fail; whether there are tongues, they will cease; whether there is knowledge, it will vanish away."***

We have looked at the beautiful family, and the question could be asked: How does Satan attack it to destroy it? The answer is simple; because we have a war in the spiritual realm (unseen world), Satan unleashed spiritual weapons such as casting spells, idolatry, magic, witchcraft, divination, infirmity, sorcery, death, against the family unit. Because of these weapons unleashed against the unit (family) in the unseen world, the end results in the seen world are family separation, homosexuality, fornication, adultery, wars, hatred, jealousy, race, sickness, poverty, violence, and death. He can also keep other people unmarried so that their God-given genealogy becomes extinct on earth. Others will die prematurely before they get married or just inmarriage that last a few days, weeks, months, or a few years; and others will get attracted to the members of the same sex (gays and lesbians). Most people will be aware of these demonic weapons yet pay less attention to their end results, which is seen in the physical world. So, when you are seeing family separation why will you be surprised and behave like nothing is happening to you and your family? Is it not the time for you to stand up and fight the devil over the family you love?

What To Do if Satan Attacks Your Health

The next strategy if Satan fails to get you through your family, is your health and the health of your other family members. This is very important for you to know. When God created your body, he created it as the temple of the Holy Spirit. This was done for communication purposes between you and God. God did not want you to know the bad part of him and he did not want you to be sick. But when humanity rebelled against him by siding with Satan, God cursed people and reduced the human lifespan to one hundred and twenty years on earth. Because of the curse, our bodies were reduced from immortality (the body that does not die and which lives on forever) to mortality (the body that breaks down and dies within 120 years). So, God had to reduce your body from the one that was pure to the one that is impure and subject to attacks by outside forces including the devil. The only way you can avoid the attack of Satan over your vulnerable body is to allow the spirit of God to sit inside you and to operate within you. When Satan comes to attack you and to live inside of you, he sees the spirit of God inside you and he flees.

Why is Your Body a Battleground Between God And Satan?

The spirits need bodies to carry out their activities in the world and particularly the bodies of the intelligent creature mankind. When God created humans, he wanted them to live closer to him and to receive orders from him. This information should be about specific instruction on how to carry out his assignment on earth. It was a mutually friendly relationship where communication was to be daily –twenty-four hours a day (24/7). As a matter of fact, humans will find it very hard to carry their God-given assignment on earth without God. And the reason is simple: without God, humans cannot understand the complicated work of God in creation. For example, the reason we go to the doctor is that we cannot understand what is happening in our bodies without them (the doctors) and their x-ray machines, that detect within our bodies what is going on with us.

When you become a believer or a Christian, you become the enemy of Satan, because he will never have your body to carry out his activities on earth. But not only in your body can you deny him, but you can also become a threat even to his existence in your family because when you discover that you have the power to stop him from destroying members of your family, he will begin to be fiercely mad at you. You can see that your freedom in Christ is also the freedom of the rest of your family members who may suffer similar attacks in future. Hence, your experience will later free them from the demonic attacks through sicknesses. Satan will attack your body through sicknesses (both curable and incurable), drug abuse, alcohol, and violence, in order to immobilise you or to kill you altogether. Once he has done this, he knows that you can become an ineffective and unproductive Christian who has nothing to contribute to the body of Christ, the church.

In the Spiritual realm (the unseen world) there is a dangerous spirit called the spirit of infirmity assigned to you to cause many illnesses that will kill or immobilise you as a Christian. The shocking truth is that many Christians do not even know that they have the power to control and keep away this spirit from attacking them. The worst-case scenario is that many Christians and to a larger extent many people of the world do not know that almost all the sicknesses are caused by spiritual powers in the spiritual realm. Well, today you have an opportunity to know in this book that you do have the power to stop these illnesses from getting to you and your family. One of the strong ways you keep these demons at bay is to keep away from sins. When you commit sin and you remain unrepentant about that sin, then you have committed lawlessness, and nothing can stop the devil from attacking you. When you commit sin, it is a rebellion against God's laws, Judgments, statutory, of which the devil will accuse you before God straightway. When you remain defiant and unrepentant, then God allows Satan to attack you because you are outside God's protection zone.

When you become sick with a life-threatening sickness, your dreams, vision and mission, strength, and your body waste away in despair, disappointment, regrets, and suicidal thoughts leading to death or living an unproductive life thereafter if you are lucky to be healed to live on. Indeed, you can see now how the devil can be deadly to you if you are a Christian. The devil is on about seeking something sinful you can commit in order to justify his attack on you and your family. ***1 Peter 5:8 says, "Be sober, be vigilant; because your adversary the devil walks about like a roaring lion, seeking whom he may devour."***

The only way you can stop the devil from attacking you is to stay away from sin as much as possible, and when you have committed one then admit it before God before Satan comes to God to accuse you of the sin. Satan cannot attack you without legal grounds such as fornication, adultery, murder, anger, jealousy, envy, offence, slander, gossips, and so much more. If you want to be free from the attack, then stay away from these things. This is not to say that the devil can only attack you through your own mistakes, he can also attack you when you have not made any mistake such as when you are helping other people in need, when there is a generational curse over your life or when you are in prayer for other people to be healed by God. But I have good news for you, they are all thwarted through the blood and the name of our Lord Jesus Christ. You have nothing to fear at all. Jesus Christ went on the cross for you and me to set us from all the sickness. Look at this beautiful verse, about how before you become sick you were healed by God. ***1 Peter 2:24 says, "who Himself bore our sins in His own body on the tree, that we, having died to sins, might live for righteousness—by whose stripes you were healed."***

This verse is telling you and me that before we became believers God had died for us and has taken away our sins. All you need to do is believe this and apply it to your sickness and you will see it disappear.

What To Do if Satan Attacks the Sources of Your Income

Satan will attack your sources of income to live a poverty ravaged life. If you have a farm, he attacks it through drought, flood, crop diseases or even a devastating regional or country war that causes you to flee your farm. At your workplace he will make sure that you stay unpromoted or he will cause hostilities between you and your bosses so that you can be sacked, or he will tempt you to have extra-marital affairs at work, or he may also cause the business to collapse, and he may even cause you to be work focussed than family focussed. He will make sure that you value your work more than your family. Why is he doing this? To make sure that you have nothing to provide for your family and to thereafter break it apart. For example, a family in which a husband is not a breadwinner is not a stable family. The woman and the children will lose respect for the husband and father who provides nothing for them. The result of the zero-income in the family is divorce, violence, hatred, jealousy, stealing, and adultery.

The biggest threat to your very existence on earth is not to have a permanent source of income. Obviously, when you do not have an income you will never live a good life here on earth. If you do not have things such as a house, clothes, food and drinks, and other luxurious properties this life needs such as gold, silver and bronze will also lead to of respect or status in the community, which we all want to have. We have confidence in the future we envisage ahead because of the properties we owned now.

The only way you can break off this cycle of poverty is to seek God. God does not only protect your life he also protects your properties and your other sources of income. God does not only protect your properties and your other sources of income he will also give you good ideas to establish your own source of income such as your permanent income-generating business. That is why the bible says, "Seek first the kingdom of God, and everything else shall be added to you". You might think I am joking but I will have you to look at this verse in the bible. **2 Chronicles 1:12. *"Wisdom and knowledge are granted to you; and I will give you riches and wealth and honour, such as none of the kings have had who were before you, nor shall any after you have the like."***

What To Do if Satan Attacks Your Relationship With Other People

While isolated from God and without God Satan will make sure that he attacks your identity by attacking your self-confidence and self-esteem. We know that people who have low self-esteem and self-confidence will never relate well with other people or even themselves. Satan will unleash the spirit of heaviness that attacks your mind and spirit of condemnation that causes nobody to appreciate your work. Once you feel rejected by other people you are reduced to your own territory of despair and loneliness. Isolated and lonely, you may begin to comfort yourself through drugs and alcohol which are deadly to your health. But not only that, when you are left with a sense of worthlessness the answer to you may be suicidal thoughts in your mind that will end your life in hell. We arrive at this thought when everything around us is falling apart or everything around us has fallen apart. We are locked in a bitterness that does not leave us alone for the rest of our life on earth. The wrong decisions we have made and the ways we are wronged by others remain forever with us and this becomes part of our daily lives. Unforgiveness against ourselves and other people who have wronged us becomes part of our culture forever. We are changed forever. Our identity is changed forever, from what it should have been to what is not us or the spiritual DNA God gave us. Life can be hopeless and meaningless without God. And indeed, to a larger extent, life can be fatal without God.

The reason we do not have the true meaning of life here on earth is that we have either abandoned God or we do not know God as our father, who has the purpose for which he created us. Knowing your purpose gives true meaning to your life. If we are to live life here on earth, it must have a sense of belonging and a sense of identity. That is why your identity and purpose in God is important to you. You were made to lead a meaningful life here on earth. That is why people who reject God try to make meaning of life by attributing humanity's existence to be from the apes. We are so confused to give a proper explanation of life and its origin that we begin to worship lifeless objects and theories such as the sun, moon, astrological theories (big bang and evolution), idols, rivers, animals. All of these are done by humans to give meaning and explanation to the lives they live and lead here on earth.

The great man of God Rick Warren put it this way; "Without God life has no purpose, and without purpose, life has no meaning. Without meaning, life has no significance or hope. We only have the true meaning of life when we know that we were created by God. What breaks my heart every day is the fact that people reject God who I know exists and speaks to me. By doing this they make themselves vulnerable to the attack by the devil if they are not already under attack by the devil and are without help from God. If we are to have our God destiny then we must seek God. If we are to know what we are created for then we must seek God. Too many wars in the world today are caused by the unfulfilled desires of our hearts. Apostle James put this very well; *James 4:1-4: Where do wars and fights come from among you? Do they not come from your desires for pleasure that war in your members? You lust and do not have. You murder and covet and cannot obtain. You fight and war. Yet you do not have because you do not ask. You ask and do not receive, because you ask amiss, that you may spend it on your pleasures. Adulterers and adulteresses! Do you not know that friendship with the world is enmity with God? Whoever therefore wants to be a friend of the world makes himself an enemy of God.*

Seeing Your Life from God's Perspective

With all the confusion in the world today, sometimes people freak out and begin to doubt God's intention for themselves and humanity at large. But I want to tell you today that despite all these dangers and the confusions we see around us- God is in control. The only way we panic sometimes about what happens to us is because we live without God or we have doubt whether God exists and has a good intention for us. This is perhaps sometimes we have no clear picture or understanding of what life on earth is all about. Well, I want to tell you now live on earth is a constant struggle. That is how God sees it, and you must see it that way too. Have you ever heard this saying; there is no permanent condition. This literally means that today is good, and tomorrow maybe bad or today is bad and tomorrow may be good. This is the mindset you should live your life with. With this mindset, nothing will overcome you easily no matter how big or small the problems may seem to be threatening your life.

The Bible is full of many histories of a constant struggle between good and bad. Life is a constant test. In fact, words such as; temptation, trials, and refining are commonly prevalent in the bible. God will allow the devil to test our character, obedience, integrity, loyalty, faith, and willingness to serve him better. Some tests may not be from God sometimes, they may be our act of foolishness in not avoiding the danger. There are some of the things we do, knowing that they are wrong, but we still do them anyway. Even as you do them nothing caught God by surprise and so when you get into danger the only solution to your problem can be God. Remember God sent us here to earth not our assignment but his assignment. That is why when we sleep too much on his assignment, he allows the devil to shake us up so we can carry out that assignment. This is all for your good I must say. While under test you will above all else seek God for answers to your problem and as that is happening your new true assignment is being given to you, while also your new character is being developed and revealed through the test. It sounds like I am inviting you to celebrate the testing of your faith, but it is your good I am telling you. The Bible is very clear on this, God wants to crown those that passed the testing of their faith with righteousness and holiness.

Now no chastening seems to be joyful for the present, but painful; nevertheless, afterwards it yields the peaceable fruit of righteousness to those who have been trained by it. **(Hebrew 12:11).**

We have seen in the Bible great people of God who were tested and passed their tests which were followed by God's blessings upon their lives. For example, people like Joseph, Ruth, Daniel, Easter, and Abraham passed their test and God was glorified through their tests. That is what God wants. He wants you to go through storms, fire, wind, and mountains so that your new character is developed and revealed which in turn brings glory to God's name. There is no one-off way in which God will test us all to develop our character, but it may come in the way of your response to your unanswered prayers, people, problems, successes, conflicts, illness, disappointment, and family tragedies. He wants to see how you will respond to these unnecessary challenges in your life. He wants to see whether you will blame him and run away from him or to come closer to him in prayers seeking answers from him.

The good news to you today is the fact that God wants you to pass your tests. Before you go into the test, he would have already given you a way to exit the test. No matter how some tests seem to overwhelm you and some tests unnoticeable there is already enough grace given for you to overcome them all. While under test you must make sure that everything that comes your way is to develop your character for the better love, peace, joy, and more importantly to be dependent upon God. He wants you to make sure that you leave your former ways for the current ways he needs in you. I personally do not wish that temptations come to you, but if they do come just be in a position to pass them with great enthusiasm because they are there for your good. God loves us all and does not seek to harm us-everything he does is for our good. You better celebrate when you are tempted than to mourn.

No temptation has overtaken you except such as is common to man; but God is faithful, who will not allow you to be tempted beyond what you are able, but with the temptation will also make the way of escape, that you may be able to bear it. (1 Corinthians 10:13).

Therefore, submit to God. Resist the devil and he will flee from you. (James 4:7)

Remember God has won the battle for you and me who believed in his son Jesus Christ. The power to defeat the Satan has been given back to us as believers, but we must always remain in Christ in order to continue to defeat Satan in this life now on earth. The only way we can defeat the Satan is to commit to the work of the cross of Jesus Christ for life. The ability to resist Satan has been given to us by God.

You can resist Satan through the weapons given to you by God such as; the name and blood of Jesus Christ, prayer, faith, truth, salvation, fasting, peace, righteousness, and confession and repentance of sins. You are a winner.

BIBLIOGRAPHY

D'Alessandro, Lauren. 2013. "Armour of God." *The you are project* 1.

Evans, Tony. 2011. *Victory in Spiritual Wafare.* Oregon: Havrvest House Publishers.

Faceforwardcolumbus. 8 March. Accessed March 8, 2021. https://faceforwardcolumbus.com.

Prince, Derek. 2015. *Blessing or Curse.* London: Derek Prince Ministeries UK.

Renner, Rick. 2015. *Dressed to Kill.* Pennsylvania: Harrison House Publishers.

Rose. "Christian Book Corporation." *Christian Book Corporation Web Site.* 3 March. Accessed March 3, 2021. https://www.christianbook.com.

Stewart, Don. 2021. "Introducing the case for Christianity." *Blue letter bible* 1.

www.ingramcontent.com/pod-product-compliance
Lightning Source LLC
Chambersburg PA
CBHW062022290426
44108CB00024B/2742